Human Relationships

David Moxon

Human Relationships

David Moxon

To my mum

Heinemann Educational Publishers
Halley Court, Jordan Hill, Oxford OX2 8EJ
a division of Reed Educational & Professional Publishing Ltd

OXFORD MELBOURNE AUCKLAND
JOHANNESBURG BLANTYRE GABORONE
IBADAN PORTSMOUTH (NH) USA CHICAGO

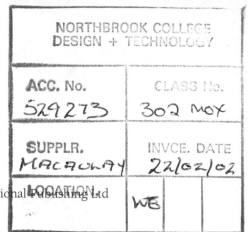

Heinemann is a registered trademark of Reed Educational & Professional Publishing Ltd

Text © David Moxon, 2001

First published in 2001

05 04 03 02 01
10 9 8 7 6 5 4 3 2 1

British Library Cataloguing in Publication Data
A catalogue record for this book is available from the British Library

ISBN 0 435 80654 8

Typeset by Wyvern 21 Ltd
Picture Research by Bob Battersby
Printed and bound in Great Britain by The Bath Press Ltd., Bath

Acknowledgements

The author would like to thank Sue Walton for all her help and encouragement on the series.

The publishers would like to thank the following for permission to reproduce copyright material: *The Guardian* for the articles on pp. 78–9 and 93; News International Limited for the articles on pp. 17, 50 and 55–6, © Times Newspapers Limited (1996, 2000 and 1999); for the article on p. 77–8, © News International Limited (2000); *Psychology Today* for fig. 2.4, p. 30, reprinted with permission from *Psychology Today* magazine, copyright © 1994, Sussex Publishers, Inc.

The publishers would like to thank the following for permission to use photographs: Paul Ekman, from the Japanese & Caucasian Facial Expressions of Emotion (JACFEE) Matsumoto and Ekman, 1988), p. 39; Giraudon, p. 28; the Harlow Primate Lab., Madison, Wisconsin, p. 17; PA photos (PA*356465), p. 78; the Victoria and Albert Museum, p. 29

The publishers have made every effort to contact copyright holders. However, if any material has been incorrectly acknowledged, the publishers would be pleased to correct this at the earliest opportunity

Cover photograph by AKG London

Tel: 01865 888058 www.heinemann.co.uk

C Contents

Introduction   vi

***Chapter 1:* Definitions and explanations of
    human relationships**   1
What are relationships?   1
Definitions   1
Interest in others – a 'natural' human
    behaviour?   2
Relationships – a 'natural' human motivation?   2
The Hierarchy of Needs   3
Multiple relationships   4
Who can we have relationships with?   4
Types of relationships   4
Research methods used in the study of
    relationships   5
Ethical and practical issues in relationship
    research   7
Evolutionary and biological explanations of
    human relationships   8
Balance theory of relationships   20
Relationships explained by learning theory   22
The economic theories of relationships   24

Real Life Applications that are considered are:
• RLA 1: Sociometry in action   7
• RLA 2: 'Smelly love' – the role of
    pheromones   11
• RLA 3: The evolution of cuddly toys   17
• RLA 4: Primitive relationships – the 'power
    of touch'   17
• RLA 5: The evolution of infidelity   20

***Chapter 2:* The development of relationships**   26
Attraction   26
Maintaining relationships   42
The breakdown of relationships   45

Real Life Applications that are considered are:
• RLA 6: The face of beauty   33
• RLA 7: Finding a partner in the personal ads   41
• RLA 8: Jealousy – a pathological condition?   50

***Chapter 3:* Intimate relationships**   52
Definitions and explanations   52
Intimate behaviours   52
Touch   52

Kissing   55
Love   56
Marriage   60
Sexual relationships   65

Real Life Applications that are considered are:
• RLA 9: The evolution of kissing   55
• RLA 10: A Zulu marriage   64
• RLA 11: Polygamy – a case study   65
• RLA 12: The 'gay gene'   69

***Chapter 4:* Contemporary issues**   74
Marriage and alternative lifestyles   74
The alternative family unit – gay couples
    adopting   76
Domestic violence   78
Child abuse   81
Incest   81
Women who 'beat' their partners   82
Women who kill their offspring   82
Rape   82
Family stress   85
Relationship therapies   88
Loneliness   90
Relationships and electronic media   91
Relationships with animals   94

Real Life Applications that are considered are:
• RLA 13: Gay couples and adoption   77
• RLA 14: Domestic violence   78
• RLA 15: Smacking children   81
• RLA 16: Rohypnol – the date rape drug   84
• RLA 17: Rape makes evolutionary sense!   85
• RLA 18: Relate – the couples counselling
    agency   88
• RLA 19: Neighbourhood loneliness   91
• RLA 20: A virtual neighbourhood   93
• RLA 21: Walking the dog – 'a good social
    exercise'   95

Advice on answering essay questions   96
Advice on answering short answer questions   98

Selected references   101

Index   103

1 Introduction

This book looks at an area of social psychology which underlies our everyday existence, human relationships. Throughout history commentators have viewed humans as 'social animals'. It has only been in recent times that researchers have begun to study interactions in a scientific way. Each chapter considers different aspects of relationships, looking at theoretical and applied concepts.

Chapter 1

This chapter begins by attempting to define relationships, then goes on to give some answers to the question 'Why do we need other people?'. Next, it outlines and evaluates a range of methods used by psychologists. Finally, a variety of explanations regarding relationships are considered.

Chapter 2

This chapter reviews the literature regarding the development of relationships. It begins by looking at the process of attraction, then attempts to define beauty. It continues with an assessment of theories of relationship maintenance. Finally, it looks at why relationships break down.

Chapter 3

This chapter is about the process and the factors involved in intimate relationships. It starts by considering intimate behaviours, next it looks at concepts of love, and different relationship styles. Finally, it looks at sexual relationships.

Chapter 4

This chapter looks at a wide range of contemporary issues. It begins by detailing a number of alternative lifestyles and goes on to consider domestic issues such as adoption by gay couples and domestic violence. Next, couples and family therapy are outlined and evaluated. Finally, three specific contemporary issues are presented: the decline in local communities; relationships with IT; relationships with pets.

How to use this book

This book has a number of features to help you understand the topic more easily. It is written to give you a wide range of skills in preparation for any of the new AS and A level psychology syllabi. Below is a list of the features with a brief summary to explain how to use them.

1 Real Life Applications

These consist of 'text boxes' which develop further a concept already discussed within the main text. Often they provide articles or outlines of studies. In all cases they attempt to apply theory to 'real life situations'.

2 Commentary

These paragraphs appear throughout the book. They follow on from issues raised within the main text. They serve a number of functions: to provide an evaluation of the earlier text, to clarify a point or to highlight some related issue. Sometimes they provide 'for' and 'against' debates.

3 Key Studies

These are descriptions of important studies within a specific area. There are two of these in each chapter. They briefly identify the aims, method, results and conclusions of the study. This feature helps you understand the methodology of research.

4 Questions

Each 'Real Life Application' has two or three short answer questions, designed to test a range of skills including: summarizing, outlining and evaluating. All of these activities are designed to allow you to acquire the 'key skills' outlined within the syllabi.

In addition, two or three 'essay style' questions are included at the end of each chapter. They specifically relate to the material covered within that chapter.

5 Advice on answering questions

At the end of the book there is a short section which gives advice on answering the essay and short answer questions.

1 Definitions and explanations of human relationships

This chapter is divided into two sections.

Section 1 begins by looking at how relationships can be defined. It then goes on to consider broader concepts such as why we are interested in others, how we are motivated to interact, and who we have relationships with. Finally, it looks at methodological and ethical issues involved in research into relationships. The following Real Life Application is considered:

- RLA 1: Sociometry in action.

Section 2 considers some of the main theoretical explanations for relationships. It starts with evolutionary explanations (which include the biological ones). Then it looks at psychosocial explanations including balance theory, learning theory (reinforcement) and economic theories (including equity and social exchange theory). Real Life Applications that are looked at are:

- RLA 2: 'Smelly love' – the role of pheromones
- RLA 3: The evolution of cuddly toys
- RLA 4: Primitive relationships – the 'power of touch'
- RLA 5: The evolution of infidelity.

SECTION 1

What are relationships?

When I began to research for this book I knew that the opening few paragraphs would be the most difficult to write. Psychologists, like philosophers, theologians and poets before them, struggle when defining the most common, universal human experience. Being a topic area within social psychology, relationships consider human behaviour within the context of interactions with others. The interactions take place along a continuum of 'closeness', a term primarily describing some sort of emotional investment. We have relationships with members of our family (theoretically the closest). Equally, we have relationships with our friends and acquaintances (these vary in closeness). In fact, the list of people who we interact with is almost endless.

Definitions

Reber (1985) divides relationships into two types: primary and secondary. Primary he describes as:

'a basic, long lasting relationship founded upon strong emotional ties and a sense of commitment to the other person'.

Secondary is described as:

'a relatively short lived relationship between persons characterised by limited interaction'.

Reber also distinguishes between the two in terms of permanence. With primary he states:

'that one member cannot simply replace the other with a new person'.

With secondary:

'they rarely have much in the way of emotional involvement

and the members in the relationship can rather easily be replaced'.

As you will see in Chapter 2 this concept of permanence is of great importance, especially when looking at breakdown and separation. If an individual emotionally invests little into a relationship, experiencing the loss of his or her partner would have little psychological impact.

The *Oxford English Dictionary* defines relationships as:

'dealings with others'.

Commentary

Definitions stress the interaction with other people, and some (as in the case of Reber's) make distinctions between levels of permanence.

Interest in others – a 'natural' human behaviour?

As you will discover throughout this book it appears that being interested in other human beings is a 'natural' human behaviour. Millions of us become 'relationship voyeurs' every day of the week, when we sit in front of the television to watch the latest episode of our favourite 'soap'. We are intrigued by the interrelationships the characters have with one another. We watch as the complexities of everyday interactions unravel before our eyes. However, this fascination with relationships extends beyond humans, even onto inanimate objects. Heider and Simmel (1944) found that adult participants readily conferred 'human characteristics' upon geometric shapes. They presented them with an animated film which depicted a large triangle, a small triangle and a small disc. They found that participants tended to describe interactions between the shapes in terms of human social relationships. Many saw the large triangle as trying to **bully** and **dominate**, whereas the disc was perceived as **timid**. Frequently the triangles were described as male and the disc female. The participants were 'seeing' human relationship behaviour in the shapes. If, as it appears, this behaviour is a 'natural' human tendency, then at what age does it first emerge?

The concept of animism

Jean Piaget (1896–1980), famous for his theories on cognitive development, suggested that from about the age of two, children spend long periods of time playing 'pretend games' bringing inanimate objects to life. They interact with cuddly toys, they talk to household objects and even describe the family car that won't start, as being 'poorly'. In this stage of cognitive development (2–7 years) children's thinking is characterized by 'animism' (Piaget, 1929). Animism can be defined as 'attributing life-like qualities to inanimate objects'.

Relationships – a 'natural' human motivation?

We have just seen that humans are pre-disposed to look for human-like behaviour in almost anything. But what of the underlying motives that 'drive' us to engage in relationships with others in the first place?

The need to be liked

Tajfel and Turner (1979) developed a theory which focused on 'social identification'. They suggested we are motivated to 'identify' with certain social groups – the so-called 'in-group'. In everyday terms this could explain why people try so hard to be liked. Some of the best social psychology is seen at parties. Most individuals spend time getting ready making themselves look good, they engage in conversations that make them look intelligent and witty and attempt to ingratiate themselves with people they perceive to be part of the 'in-group'.

Harre (1979) suggested one of the major human social motivations is the avoidance of 'social humiliation'. As the above example suggests, most of us try very hard to be accepted by our immediate social circles and to a larger extent by society as a whole. When we feel foolish or stupid, or when relationship disharmony has occurred, we are motivated to try to 'correct' the situation. Reconciliation techniques are seen in many higher level species including apes (De Waal, 1989) If we really care for the relationship we will do all we can to re-establish it.

The motivation to fulfil needs

Much of the early work into motivation theory assumed that we all possess 'instinctual drives' which allow us to fulfil fundamental needs. Extending McClelland's (1951) work looking at 'need for achievement', McAdams (1982) developed a framework which detailed two 'motivations' within the context of relationships. He suggested we are 'driven' to seek out rewarding relationships with a number of people (the need for affiliation). Secondly, we seek warm close relationships (because of our need for intimacy). People vary in the level of fulfilment they receive. Those who have their need for 'intimacy' met, frequently experience a higher level of trust and intimacy in their relationships, than those who have their 'affiliation needs met' more often (McAdams and Bryant, 1987). Some people prefer to have lots of friends and acquaintances (a wide circle of friends) while others only have one or two very close friends.

Argyle (1967) proposed that relationships fulfil eight fundamental needs within us. Table 1.1 summarizes them and highlights people who could potentially be associated with their fulfilment.

As can be seen from Table 1.1, many people can be associated with a specific need. Some people can

Table 1.1: Relationship needs and people who fulfil them

Need	Associated person(s)
Biological needs (food, drink, warmth, etc.)	Mother (or other surrogate care-giver) Family members in general Carer (in the case of disabled people) Self (in the case of independent adults) Sexual partner
Dependency (help, support, protection, etc.)	Mother (or other surrogate care-giver) Family members in general Carer (in the case of disabled people) Sexual partner Teacher Priest Doctor Employer
Affiliation (social acceptance)	Mother (or other surrogate care-giver) Family members in general Close friends Priest
Dominance (a need to be in charge)	Our children Subordinates at work Maybe our sexual partners!
Sex	Sexual partner
Aggression (a need to hurt others – could be physically or psychologically)	Neighbours Family members in general Close friends Employer Subordinates at work Our children Sexual partner
Self-esteem (the need to feel good about ourselves)	Sexual partner Potentially anyone who shows us love and respect
Other motivations (these include money, interests beliefs, etc.)	Potentially anyone who reinforces these factors

fulfil numerous needs within us, and for that reason they take on a special significance. Mothers and sexual partners are two such people.

Commentary

All the theories regarding motivation stem from a basic assumption that humans are 'driven' (by primitive instincts) to fulfil certain requirements. This idea originated in the work of people such as McDougall (1932), who believed that the presence of a drive could be inferred by the outward behaviour of an organism. Later, in 1967, Grossman made a distinction between 'internally' and 'externally' elicited drives. Biological drives such as hunger, etc. come from an internal imbalance, whereas sexual behaviour and socialization stem from an external source (environmental cues). During the 1950s and 1960s Maslow had attempted to produce a comprehensive theory which incorporated both.

The Hierarchy of Needs

In 1954, Abraham Maslow presented his theory, the 'Hierarchy of Needs'. In it he suggested that humans are intrinsically motivated to progress through a series of stages, as each set of needs are fulfilled (see Figure 1.1). He suggested that we share the lower needs with all other living species (physiological and safety). However, love, feelings of belongingness and self-esteem are only shared with species that possess 'higher levels of consciousness'. He viewed self-actualization as a uniquely human achievement. So for Maslow, seeking the company

Figure 1.1: Maslow's Hierarchy of Needs

of others and engaging in relationships with them is a fundamental 'human need'.

Multiple relationships

Shaffer and Emmerson (1964) were the first to propose that young children are able to form affectionate bonds with more than one person – the so-called 'multiple attachment theory'. We carry this ability throughout our childhood and into adult life. Imagine what life would be like if you could only form a friendship with one person at a time! To emphasize this point further, I often suggest to students that they write down the 'top five' people in their life. I tell them it must be in order of affection. Of course, this is an impossible task, because for most of us, we will have three or four people, at least, vying for first place. However, this illustration does make two useful points. It shows that we are able to have 'multiple relationships' and also that these relationships are of different types.

Who can we have relationships with?

As we have already seen, we form relationships with numerous people. It is only quite recently that psychologists have interested themselves in what could be termed more 'traditional relationships'. Much of the early work focused on interpersonal attraction (almost exclusively heterosexual) and highlighted factors that influenced initial liking. About the same time (the early 1960s), attachment theory was breaking new grounds, especially the mother – child bond. Two social psychologists Ellen Berscheid and Elaine Hatfield published the first major text on interpersonal attraction in 1969. In it they attempted to tackle not only attraction theory but also theories of love and the development, maintenance and breakdown of relationships. This was pioneering work as it involved looking at topics that, until then, had been within the domain of sociologists, counsellors and anthropologists. Since the 1970s, this broadening of approach and co-operation with other disciplines, has meant that psychologists can study a wide range of relationships.

Contemporary research looks at alternative relationships (including homosexual couples and homosexual families), employer/employee relations and grandparent/grandchild interactions (to name a few), all areas that until very recently had been heavily neglected.

Types of relationships

If we hold positive attitudes towards another person we are said to 'like' them. Many relationships are based on this notion. Often they are 'secondary' (in Reber's definition on p. 1), because our contact with the other person is minimal and less deep.

If we hold 'strong emotional' feelings towards another person (primary in Reber's definition) we are said to 'love' them. Rubin (1973) suggests love has three components:

- Attachment – we feel the need to be physically close to the person.
- Caring – we feel responsible for their well-being.
- Intimacy – we feel able to express our deepest thought and feelings. (We will consider love in more detail in Chapter 3.)

Same-sex relationships

Research has shown that on the whole women's same-sex friendships tend to be based on 'emotional sharing', whereas men's tend to be based on sharing activities and common interests (Sharrod, 1989).

Commentary

However, psychologists such as Duck and Wright (1993) argue that this gender difference is too simplistic. We must remember, individuals will be influenced by many factors in the 'public expression' of their relationships. Peer pressure and society's attitudes all contribute to how friends behave in public. In Britain, 'real men' don't cry or talk about emotions with their mates, and they don't cuddle in public (unless they are footballers). It is more acceptable for women to express their emotions within the context of same-sex relationships.

'Exchange and Communal' relationships

Clark and Mills (1979) originally developed a way of classifying relationships based upon their type. They proposed two fundamental types: 'Exchange and Communal'. In Exchange, the individuals involved expect an immediate benefit for any investment: 'I do something for you – you do something for me' – a quid-pro-quo arrangement. Communal relationships, on the other hand, are based on the philosophy of 'giving without keeping a score'. The idea of a communal ethos is explored in more detail in Chapter 4, when we look at communes (p. 75).

Commentary

So are Communal type relationships really the opposite of Exchange, or do benefits occur in more subtle ways? Clark and Mills (1993) make the point 'that not all satisfactions or rewards that derive from relationships are benefits'. A person may receive great satisfaction from 'looking after' (loving) someone else. That person, in turn, may thoroughly enjoy 'being looked after' (receiving love). So who is getting what out of this relationship? On the face of it, it may appear imbalanced, however, both are happy (certainly in the short term). This whole concept of 'equity' is looked at in more detail on p. 25.

Research methods used in the study of relationships

Because research into relationships is studied as part of the wider topic of social psychology the methods used come in many different shapes and forms. Many psychologists make a distinction between 'basic research', which contributes towards generating theories, and 'applied research', which applies theory to naturally occurring events, and seeks to create solutions to social problems (Cook *et al*,1985). Regardless of whether the research is basic or applied, a wide range of methodologies is used. It would be unrealistic to attempt to explain all the techniques used, otherwise this book would become a research methods book. Outlined below are four of the more interesting used in the study of relationships.

1 Self report

As the name implies participants are required to disclose their thoughts or feelings regarding some issue. Often, this could require them to rate someone in terms of their appearance. Another, useful measure, particularly when looking at relationships, could be self-esteem. How are self-report questionnaires actually constructed? Let us now look at two widely used methods.

The Likert Scale

This system was developed and consequently named after Rensis Likert (1932), and is used primarily in the measurement of attitudes. The researcher firstly identifies an equal number of negative and positive statements about an issue, and participants are requested to rate these statements using the following scale:

Strongly agree	Agree	Undecided	Disagree	Strongly disagree
5	4	3	2	1

The researcher then totals the responses for each question (or item), and an overall attitude score is obtained. Clearly, the higher the score the more agreement with the statements has been shown.

Commentary

A test of discrimination is carried out on each item, to assess how useful each question is. This is a strength of using Likert Scales as it means that individual questions can be checked against overall judgements. Studies have found that compared to other measures of attitude, the Likert Scale scores higher on reliability (Edwards and Kinney, 1946) and also for ease of question writing (Nunnally, 1976). Weaknesses of this method include problems with people choosing the middle position on the scale (undecided). When given the option many people choose to 'sit on the fence'. Another problem is that the researcher is deciding what questions are asked.

A number of researchers have taken the Likert Scale and modified it to apply to relationships. Probably the best known of these is Rubin's (1970) scale to assess liking and love. In an interesting study which combined both self-report questionnaire and 'covert observation' (see p. 6), Rubin (1973) observed couples waiting to complete his questionnaire. He predicted that the amount of time they spent gazing into each other's eyes would correspond to the score they obtained on the 'love questionnaire'. This is exactly what was found. High scoring couples on the love scale spent significantly more time gazing at one another than those whose scores were lower.

The Semantic Differential

This scale was developed by Osgood *et al* (1957). It is used primarily to assess individual's perceptions of particular issues. The participants are asked to mark a position between two 'bipolar adjectives':

Attractive	_ _ ✔ _ _ _ _ _ _ _	Unattractive
Rugged	✔ _ _ _ _ _ _ _ _ _	Delicate
Pleasant	_ ✔ _ _ _ _ _ _ _ _	Unpleasant

Commentary

The Semantic Differential 'apparently' produces good reliability values and correlates well with other attitude scales (Coolican, 1994). There is the tendency for participants to use the extremes of the scale. Even though this also occurs on the Likert Scales, it is more of a problem here because there are no headings explaining each position (agree, strongly agree, etc.). Another weakness, again the same as Likert Scales, is that the experimenter chooses the adjectives in the first place.

Rather than using questionnaires to elicit participants' attitudes towards issues, some researchers choose more informal methods such as 'narrative materials'. Here the participants may use diaries or keep notes, over a period of time. The researcher then develops a coding system based upon the issue/s that are being looked at. One common area of research for this method is close relationships (e.g. Harvey *et al*,1992).

Commentary

Two problems using narrative methods are: firstly, there is little consistency between research – each researcher is developing his or her own 'scoring system' (method of coding); secondly, there is little control over what participants choose to write about. This makes comparisons between participants very difficult. However, it must be stressed that some academics see this point as a strength rather than a weakness. Participants are free to explore issues which they see as important, rather than being forced into 'pigeon hole' answers as is often the case with questionnaires.

A general problem with all self-report methods is that there is a tendency for people to present themselves in a favourable way. Some research has shown however that if participants believe that their responses can be checked by some 'infallible lie detector', levels of 'truth telling' can increase (e.g. Aguinis *et al*, 1993). If participants believe their answers can be verified, they are more likely to give more truthful responses.

2 Observations

Another very frequently used technique in social psychology is the observation. Many animal studies use observational methods as their research tool. If a researcher was interested in non-verbal communication (NVC) of couples on a first date, one obvious technique to employ would be to watch them. Arguably one of the earliest scientific attempts to measure attraction was proposed by Francis Galton in 1884. He suggested:

'when two persons have an inclination to one another, they visibly incline or slope together when sitting side by side'.

He goes on to say:

'It does not require much ingenuity to arrange a pressure gauge with an index and dial to indicate changes in stress'.

One further point he makes is that it is difficult to achieve without being noticed. Galton's observa-

tions however are still relevant today. Commentators on NVC talk about 'mirroring' which is where couples who are getting on particularly well orientate their posture towards each other, often appearing as mirror images (Pease, 1981).

There are four types of observation possible. Participant observation is where the researcher actually takes part in the research itself. This is extremely difficult in relationship studies, because by becoming personally involved, objectivity is severely reduced. Non-participant observation is the most useful as the researcher observes from a distance, and therefore should have no effect on the behaviour being observed. The third type of observation is discrete (or covert), where the participant(s) are unaware they are being watched. Clearly, there are many ethical issues arising here, but as a research tool it is very useful because the participants will behave more naturally. The fourth method is overt observation where it is clear the participants are being watched.

Commentary

Observations are a useful technique for social psychologists to study relationships. However, even with high 'inter-rater reliability' (agreement between different raters watching the same phenomenon), overall objectivity is still poor. One way of addressing this is to carry out observational studies using machines. An interesting piece of research was carried out in the mid-1970s, which attempted to discover objectively whether males became more sexually aroused than females in the presence of erotic material. The overriding assumption prior to this research was that males became more stimulated than females. Ironically most of this evidence had come from self reports. Julia Heiman (1977) played tape recordings of erotic stories to her participants, while measuring their levels of sexual arousal using a 'penile strain gauge' (to measure male arousal) and a 'photoplethysmograph' (to measure female arousal). She found that contrary to popular believe both male and female responses to erotic material were quite similar, but that women were sometimes unaware of their own physiological arousal.

3 The survey

Within the context of relationships, the survey method can be a very useful tool. Researchers can ask a vast number of people questions about the sort of person they are attracted to, what they look for in relationships and how they cope when it all goes wrong. One of the most wide-ranging and notorious surveys was conducted by Kinsey (1948, 1953) into American sexual behaviour. In the 1993 November/December issue of *Psychology Today* (an American 'popular magazine'), researchers asked readers to help identify how contemporary men and women perceive and value male appearance. Over 1500 people responded, with 64 per cent of them being women. This survey gave the authors an opportunity to gauge the US public's opinions on this interesting social issue (Pertshuk *et al*, 1994). The results to this study can be found in Chapter 2 (Fig. 2.5, p. 31).

Commentary

Surveys are constructed in such a way as to make them easy to analyse. In most cases this involves either generating percentage scores (e.g. 42 per cent of women like tall men, etc.) or asking participants to rank certain factors (as in the case of Pertshuk *et al*'s study). Another advantage with surveys is that many participants can be questioned fairly quickly. Disadvantages of surveys include a risk that participants will give answers they think they ought to give (social desirability) and large-scale surveys can be expensive to administer.

4 Sociometry

This is a method used by social psychologists to help analyse social interactions. One of its major advantages is that it is clear in showing who likes who in social groups. It is therefore useful at identifying 'social isolates' and those individuals who are very popular. RLA 1 gives an example of a 'directed graph' between seven people.

Summary

- Sociometry allows us to represent liking and reciprocation of that liking.
- It is a useful technique to identify popular and isolated members of groups.
- One drawback of sociometry is that it gives no indication of levels of liking.

Questions

1 Who are the most popular people at the party?

2 Is anyone socially isolated?

3 Give two examples where 'reciprocal liking' is not evident.

Commentary

Sociometry gives researchers an overview of social situations. Its usage as a method is therefore limited. Two further problems with this technique are that it is rather simplistic and it can get very complicated depending on how many people are involved and the nature of their relationships.

Ethical and practical issues in relationship research

Because of the nature of research into relationships a number of ethical considerations need to be considered. Firstly, there is a tendency that researchers will bring their own prejudices and cultural biases to their research hypotheses. As Medawar (1967) astutely points out:

'There is no such thing as an unbiased observation.'

This becomes an issue if a researcher believes he or she has 'a monopoly on the truth'. In other words, there is a normal pattern of relationship behaviour, and any deviation from it is dysfunctional. As we will see in Chapter 3, research into marriage takes a modern, western position as 'the norm'.

Real Life Application 1:

Sociometry in action

Seven people have come together for a dinner party at Mike's house. Some of the people know each other, some do not. As psychologists, we are interested in the interactions that take place. The arrows in Figure 1.2 indicate the direction of liking. Observe the interactions carefully, then answer the questions below.

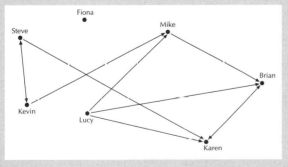

Figure 1.2: A fictitious example of a sociogram

Deception

Another important ethical issue that frequently arises in social research is the issue of deception. Should participants be aware that they are taking part in a study? Clearly, knowing that you are being watched and assessed, encourages you to change your behaviour. Orne (1962) referred to these changes as 'demand characteristics'. Two examples of this are:

- pleasing the experimenter – participants try to do as they think they should
- evaluation apprehension – knowing you are being assessed causes anxiety. It is this which causes changes in behaviour.

Work by Masling (1966) into pleasing the experimenter found that in many cases the opposite effect is observed. Many participants do the opposite of what they think the participant requires of them.

Observing in public places

To what extent should psychologists be allowed to observe people in public places? David Givens, an anthropologist, has spent many hours observing couples in singles bars in America. He has developed interesting theories regarding 'chat-up' lines and sexual NVC signals, without people realizing they were part of his experiments (Givens, 1983).

Commentary

The British Psychological Society's Guidelines (1994) suggest that it is acceptable to observe people 'going about their everyday lives'. In public they would expect to be observed. It would be a slightly different matter if a psychologist climbed up a drainpipe and observed a couple in the privacy of their own home!

Practical issues

One obvious problem with studying relationships is analysing their development over time. Longitudinal studies are notoriously tricky, with people dropping out half way through, not to mention the expense of resourcing such work. Another problem is the lack of variety in the types of relationships studied. In 1978, Huston and Levinger argued that there were predominantly three types of social relationship studied:

- relationships of people roughly the same age and sex
- relationships of people of the opposite sex (romantic types)

- relationships within marriage.

As was pointed out earlier, things are changing but there is still a long way to go before a balance is reached.

True to life?

Many studies (particularly the older ones) rely on showing participants photographs to judge their attractiveness. Clearly, we judge people 'in the flesh' in real life, therefore 'ecological validity' must be questioned.

Commentary

As we saw earlier, the work of people such as Givens (1983) in singles bars overcomes these difficulties. His work is naturalistic, because it is conducted in the field. However, this has its drawbacks, primarily because of the lack of control.

Cross-cultural research

Berscheid (1985) suggested that the majority of research into sexual attraction has been based upon American college students. Clearly, unless you fit this category it may be dubious to generalize findings. Moghaddam *et al* (1993) argue that Western culture seems to produce relationships that are based upon 'individuality', whereas non-Western cultures tend to stress 'collectiveness'. This could imply that 'relationship rewards' may be fundamentally different for different cultures (see p. 00).

SECTION 2

Evolutionary and biological explanations of human relationships

Humans as animals

Referring to a human as an animal is a legacy from Darwinian theory, and one that modern scientists still believe to be true. As children, we are taught that humans evolved from the apes. For this reason we are nothing more than mentally sophisticated chimpanzees. But this assertion must have implications for our experiences. We possess primitive underlying behaviours, which at some level must influence who we are today. Evolutionary ideas attempt to identify these 'primitive drives' and relate them to modern behaviour.

In more recent years there has been a growing interest in explaining human behaviour in terms of its evolutionary benefits. This division of the discipline has become known as 'evolutionary psychology'. According to Buss (1999) evolutionary psychology focuses on four key questions:

1 Why is the mind designed the way it is?
2 How is the mind designed?
3 What is the mind designed to do?
4 How does our current environment affect our primitively developed mind?

Let us take each of these questions in turn and see how they attempt to explain relationship behaviour.

1 Why is the mind designed the way it is?

Social animals

Scientists have always made the assumption that humans are 'social animals' rather than solitary creatures. But what are the benefits of being sociable? As will be seen throughout this book the psychological (and indeed health) benefits of being in a happy relationship almost go without saying. Having people around us allows us to share our feelings, gives us emotional support and allows us the opportunity to feel loved and wanted. We have no reason to believe that our ancient ancestors didn't value these qualities also. However, to them, being sociable had more practical advantages as well.

The evolution of co-operation

Co-operation refers to 'working together to achieve some common goal'. For our ancestors this could have included hunting and protection.

Types of societies

Archaeologists tend to agree that our earliest ancestors lived a 'hunter-gatherer' existence. This combination of hunting meat and gathering plant material is unique to humans as a subsistence strategy (Leakey, 1994). These pre-historical 'societies' consisted of small groups or tribes of people (possibly about 25), in which co-operation between members of the group was of paramount importance.

Hunting

Archaeological sites of 'Homo erectus' (a forerunner of modern humans) have strongly suggested they were hunters of big game such as elephants (Elephas antiquus – now extinct). They would have worked in groups to plan and execute their attacks. Group work was vital if such huge prey were to be caught. Figure 1.3 illustrates some of these co-operative strategies.

Commentary

The concept of 'hunting' as the foundation of human socialization took on even greater significance, when Isaac, a Harvard University archaeologist, published a landmark paper in *Scientific American* in 1978. He suggested that it wasn't hunting behaviour itself which accelerated human evolution, but the interaction around the sharing of the food. The 'sharing hypothesis' as it became known, meant that behaviours such as social reciprocity, intelligence and the development of language were given a 'kick start' by engaging in 'communal eating'. There is still much debate as to when language emerged within our species, but clearly this would have had a major impact.

Hunting in the modern world

Within the last couple of hundred years the so-called 'modern world' has emerged. It developed as a bi-product of the Industrial Revolution. As more everyday processes became mechanized, the need for agricultural labour reduced. Today, less than

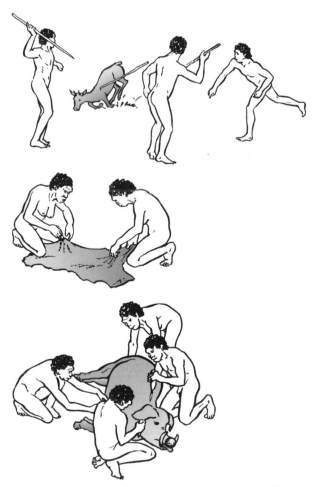

Figure 1.3: Examples of co-operation strategies in early hominids

2 per cent of the British population works in agriculture. The population within modern industrialized societies lives within 'dense groupings', a far cry from our hunter-gatherer roots. The need to hunt for food has disappeared in modern Westernized societies. If we want to eat we pay a visit to the local supermarket, or the local fast-food outlet.

Commentary

Some commentators propose that mealtimes, as an example of family togetherness, are under threat because of the emphasis today upon fast food and convenience catering. Taking this argument further, Beardsworth and Keil (1993) have suggested that food is not a 'nutritional exercise', but food and eating play vital roles in articulating social relations, as well. In his book *Britain on the couch* (1998), clinical psychologist Oliver James suggests our 5-million-year-old genes are not particularly suited for modern, 'high-tech' lifestyles.

As we have just seen, a major benefit to our ancestors living in social groups would have been their ability to hunt more effectively. All planning and hunting strategies would have required co-operation. However, co-operation would also have allowed them to develop strategies for protection. Living in groups (or alliances) would have increased their chances of survival against predators (particularly when those predators would be other tribes of Homo sapiens – humans).

2 How is the mind designed?

In this section we will look at a range of evolutionary and biological factors that contribute to make us receptive to relationships. In many ways these form the 'nuts and bolts' of relationship behaviour. We will consider the following factors:

- body shape
- pheromones
- hormones
- attachment.

Attraction of body shape

One of the more controversial evolutionary theories attempted to relate females' body shape to their sexual attractiveness to members of the opposite sex. Devendra Singh (1993) published his findings in the academic journal *Nature*. He suggested that although Western ideals of 'beautiful female bodies' had changed over the past 50 years (primarily becoming lighter and thinner), their waist–hip ratio

had remained relatively constant. This calculation was achieved by dividing the waist measurement by the hip size (including the buttocks). Singh proposed that the lower the waist–hip ratio the more sexually attractive the woman becomes. In evolutionary terms Singh believes this can be explained in terms of fat distribution. During puberty, young women deposit more fat on their hips which not only gives them a more rounded 'hour glass' figure, but also a much lower waist–hip ratio compared to males. It is of course during this time that females are 'ready' to bear children. After the female menopause the waist–hip ratio changes, becoming much more similar to males.

Commentary

Singh's work clearly suggests that nature has 'designed' the female body to signal fertility. The more curvaceous the female, the more likely she is to bear offspring. Indeed more recent evidence collected from fertility clinics suggests women with a lower waist–hip ratio get pregnant quicker than women whose waist–hip ratios are higher (cited in Buss, 1999). Also, when a woman is ovulating the increase in oestrogen produces an observable decrease in her waist–hip ratio (cited in Symons, 1995). However, it must be remembered that as with all evolutionary explanations, they are only relevant to heterosexual relationships.

The role of pheromones

Pheromones are chemical substances used as a form of communication between members of a species. They are primarily involved in signalling sexual responsiveness, alarm and territoriality. Unlike 'endocrine hormones' (which are secreted directly into the bloodstream), pheromones are secreted outside the body. This means that olfaction (smell) is the sense of detection.

A lot of the early research in this field was conducted on laboratory mice. Powerful sexual responses were discovered. For example, exposing a female mouse to male urine induces ovulation and sexual responsiveness. However, if the male mouse has been castrated, then its urine will have no effect (Bruce, 1969). Pheromone effects have been identified in other animals including rats, dogs, stallions, bulls and rams (Michael and Keverne, 1968).

Some studies have looked at pheromone responses in primates. Herbert (1966) found that oestrogen treatment of a female rhesus monkey sexually aroused the male monkeys with whom she shared a cage. Blocking the males' sense of smell significantly reduced this arousal.

What are the benefits of pheromones?

One of the most well-documented benefits of animal pheromones is their reproductive advantage. A rodent's urine differs in odour, according to what type of major histocompatibility complex (MHC) genes it has. These genes are involved in developing immune system functioning. A rodent who selects a sexual partner with a different combination of genes to its own, will increase its chances of producing more 'immunologically robust' offspring. It appears that by smelling the 'immunlogical signature' of their partners, rodents can enhance their reproductive pedigree.

Human pheromones?

Despite all the research identifying animal pheromones, there is still much debate whether a human pheromone exists. In the 1970s McClintock was the first to show that the menstrual cycles of women who spent a lot of time together can synchronize. In two series of studies she tested this hypothesis. In the first she took a swab from female volunteers' armpits, removed any odour, then wiped the remaining tasteless and odourless liquid onto the lips of other female volunteers. Within a few months the pairs of women had 'periods' that were synchronized. In the second, male volunteers

had armpit swabs taken. The process of deodourising was used, as in the first series of studies, and the liquid was 'wiped' on the lips of female volunteers who had irregular menstrual cycles. Repeated exposure to the male secretions caused the periods to become more regular.

A question frequently asked is, 'Is it possible to synthesize artificially a substance that acts as a sexual attractant?'. Can pheromones be bottled? Real Life Application 2 looks at this issue.

Summary

- Companies are investing money into trying to find a 'chemical attractant'.
- Studies have found that exposure to artificial pheromones induces sexual responses in a number of animal species.
- Academics such as Meredith Small (1999) suggest that human sexuality is too complex to be totally affected by chemical stimulation. She argues factors such as culture and family play key roles.

Questions

1 What are pheromones?

2 Apart from the two cited in the article, what other reasons could make pheromones less effective in humans than in other animal species?

Real life Application 2:

'Smelly love' – the role of pheromones

David Berliner of 'Pherin' California claims that his company has produced two colognes based on human pheromones – one for men and one for women. His suggestion is that these colognes are designed to make the wearer feel more relaxed and self confident. Does this mean that in the future the choice of sexual partner will be determined by chemistry in a bottle? Small (1999), professor of anthropology at Cornell University thinks not. She points out we are a behaviourally fickle species, and swayed by factors such as culture and family when it comes to finding a mate. The idea of an instantaneous 'sexual attractant' for humans is still in the realms of science fiction.

Article adapted from *Your bionic future* – a *Scientific American* supplement, 1999.

The role of hormones

Hormones are substances which act as 'chemical messengers', sending and delivering information around the body. In this section we will concentrate upon the 'endocrine' system, the internal hormonal communication system. But what has this got to do with relationships? We stated earlier that all evolutionary explanations of behaviour focused upon the underlying mechanisms. By understanding them, the argument goes, we will understand the purpose of the behaviour itself. Hormones, regulate every aspect of behaviour, including relationship experiences.

Let us now look at some hormonal influences.

a   The sex hormones

If you think back to biology lessons, you probably recall being taught about the sex hormones testosterone, oestrogen and progesterone. The influence of these hormones begins at conception. The sex chromosomes an individual acquires at fertilization trigger the production of each of these hormones. If the embryo is XX (female), she will produce predominantly female hormones and will develop into a girl. If the embryo is male (XY), male hormones will be produced in large quantities and a boy will develop. At about six weeks, the sexually ambiguous embryo starts to differentiate, and develop the appropriate genitalia for its sex.

b   Sexual disorders

Very rarely this prenatal hormonal exposure can go wrong. When this happens individuals are born with ambiguous reproductive structures, a condition referred to as 'hermaphroditism'. An example of this is known as 'Androgen Insensitivity Syndrome'. Genetic males (XY) produce the correct levels of testosterone (an androgen), however because their tissues are 'insensitive' to its effects, subsequent development is feminized. Individuals with this condition appear female. Money and Ehrhardt (1972) spent many years researching these abnormal conditions and described numerous case studies. A question which consistently intrigued them was, to what extent did an individual's concept of their gender relate to their 'biological' programming. Do we learn appropriate sex-related behaviour from the environment or is it created through our genes and hormones? Money suggests that humans are 'psychosexually' neutral at birth, and that a concept of gender is produced by learning and the environment. If a hermaphrodite baby undergoes reassignment surgery (that is removal of the inconsistent genitalia) it must take place very soon after birth. After 18 months severe psychological adjustment problems occur, as around this age a young child is just starting to develop a sense of their own gender identity (Kohlberg, 1966; Money and Ehrhardt, 1972).

Commentary

Reproductive biologist Milton Diamond (1965, 1982) criticizes Money's environmental position in determining 'gender identity'. He cites cases reported by Money where reassignment surgery appeared to be successful during childhood, however problems arose during adolescence. While acknowledging environmental factors Diamond suggests that 'gender-related behaviour' is being 'driven' by biological influences. More evidence for Diamond's position came from a rather bizarre study of a small community in the Dominican Republic called the 'Guevodoces'. It was reported by Imperato-McGinley et al (1974), writing in the academic journal Science. Due to a very rare hormonal condition (referred to as Alpha-5 Reductase Syndrome), many genetic males were born who appeared to be females. Because their parents were unaware of this they were socialised as female. However, at puberty, hormonal changes caused a penis to develop, and the children became male. At this point their behaviour appeared to change also. They became masculine and they developed heterosexual interests. Years of socialization as females could not 'stem' the influence of biology upon gender behaviour.

So the sex hormones we possess, determine the sex we develop into. As we have just seen, occasionally this process goes wrong. Clearly, our sex has a major impact upon our everyday relationships. The next question we need to ask is, 'How do hormones influence sexual behaviour itself?'.

c   Hormone and sex behaviour

Hormones not only play a vital role in 'organizing' our sexual organs, but they are also involved in activating the sexual response (the so-called 'organizing/activating role (Feder, 1984)). It has been well documented over the years that if a male laboratory rat or mouse is castrated (has its testes removed – therefore removing its source of testosterone) it will cease engaging in sexual behaviour and be less aggressive. If at a later stage testosterone is reintroduced via injections, normal sexual behaviour will resume. Clearly a major problem with animal studies centres around their applicability to humans. 'Lower species' are influenced much more directly by their biochemistry. Humans are more influenced by learning and past experiences.

Hormones and human research

A study was conducted by Udry et al (1985) in which they questioned the sexual behaviour of boys in the 8th, 9th and 10th grades of an American school. They correlated the results they obtained from blood samples measuring levels of testosterone. What was found was a relationship between increased sexual behaviour (sexual intercourse and masturbation) and higher levels of testosterone. This finding was completely independent of age. The authors concluded that during puberty, levels of sexual behaviour are directly affected by testosterone levels.

Commentary

Studies such as Udry *et al*'s (1985) illustrate that there is a direct link between hormonal levels, and the corresponding outward behaviour. Does this imply therefore, that because men and women differ in their 'hormonal makeup', they will inevitably differ in their behaviours?

d Brain differences between males and females

In a study conducted by Phoenix *et al* (1959) and reported in the journal *Endocrinology*, female guinea pigs were artificially exposed to testosterone prenatally (before they were born). In adulthood they failed to show appropriate female sexual behaviour. It was concluded that prenatal exposure to testosterone had 'organized' brain tissue in a 'male' orientation. Similar results were found in male rats, but in the opposite direction. When they were castrated at birth, and given female hormones at adulthood, they showed female sexual behaviour patterns. The researchers in this study (Harris and Levine, 1965) proposed that castration at birth had 'sensitized' these male rat brains into a 'female orientation', and at adulthood, the artificial administration of female hormones had 'activated' the 'female behaviour patterns'.

Once again, we find ourselves falling into the trap of relying on animal studies in an attempt to explain human behaviour. However, there is plenty of evidence within the scientific literature to suggest hormones lead men and women to think differently. It is well documented that regular changes in personality correlate with phases of the menstrual cycle (Bardwick, 1971). During the first phase of the menstrual cycle, increasing levels of oestrogen stimulate neural cells, which in turn gives rise to feelings of contentment and pleasure. In the second phase progesterone levels increase. These are associated with neural inhibition, and the resultant behaviours include anxiety, tiredness and depression. In the third phase, a few days before menstruation occurs both hormone levels decrease drastically. The resultant behaviour manifests itself in rapid mood changes and hypersensitivity. Clearly, women vary in how sensitive they are to these 'hormonal swings'. A study cited in Stone (1982) found that more than half of the female acute psychiatric and medical admissions were made during the pre-menstrual or menstrual period. Evolution appears to have equipped women with an evolutionary timetable that makes them experience pleasure and content-

ment, when they are most likely to conceive (Moir and Jessel, 1989).

Commentary

The legal profession views hormonal influences on behaviour as a 'plea' in its own right. If a mother was to kill her baby within one year and one day she can make a plea of 'infanticide', which incurs a far less severe penalty than first degree murder. In French law 'premenstrual tension' (PMT) is placed within the same category as 'temporary insanity'. Even though British law doesn't quite go this far, the PMT defence has twice been successfully pleaded in Britain, reducing murder charges to manslaughter, therefore incurring a lesser penalty (cited in Moir and Jessel, 1989).

e Oxytocin – the relationship hormone?

The role of oxytocin in reproductive behaviour has been well documented within mammals. Within humans it stimulates milk ejection during lactation, uterine contractions during childbirth and is released during orgasm in both men and women. Recently scientists at the University of California, San Francisco have shown an association with the hormone oxytocin and the ability to maintain 'healthy interpersonal relationships with others'. Rebecca Turner (lead author of the study) suggests that 'oxytocin may be mediating emotional experiences in close relationships' (Turner *et al*, 1999). Two important findings have emerged from their study. Firstly, women who were currently involved in a committed relationship showed greater oxytocin increases to positive emotional stimuli than single women. Secondly, having 'enough' oxytocin available during 'negative experiences' can help in reducing their effects.

Commentary

Studies such as Turner *et al*'s (1999), illustrate how interrelated evolutionary and biological explanations are. She goes on to conclude that: 'it makes sense that during pregnancy and postpartum (after birth), both a woman's body and her mind will be stimulated to nurture her child'. As men do not produce the same levels of oxytocin it is interesting to speculate where this leaves them in the 'relationship game'. It is a fact that some commentators believe that men and women require fundamentally different things out of relationships. Probably one of the best known of these is the author of *Men are from Mars, women are from Venus* (Gray, 1992). However, we must be careful not to assume that these proposed sex differences are explained through biology alone. Social experiences can adjust levels of hormones.

Fathers can learn through social experience to be just as emotionally close to their offspring as mothers.

Attachment – the concept of a secure base

One of the pioneers of attachment theory was Mary Ainsworth *et al* (1978). Through her highly controlled observations of interactions between infants and mothers she developed a reliable method of assessing the 'strength' and 'type' of relationship between mother and child. She distinguished three patterns of attachment: secure and two types of insecure (see Key Study 1). A very important feature of securely attached infants was their use of 'mother' as a secure base. They would explore new surroundings, but keep looking back to check that mum was still there. If they became anxious or distressed they made a hasty return to their mothers.

KEY STUDY 1

Researchers: Ainsworth, Blehar, Waters and Wall (1978)

Aims: The aim of the study was to identify patterns of attachment behaviour in infants.

Method: The researchers used the 'strange situation' which involved putting children through a series of eight episodes within a strange room. Their behaviour was recorded by trained observers. Each episode consisted of approximately three minutes, with the baby sometimes being left with the mother, sometimes with a stranger and sometimes on their own.

Results: Three discrete patterns of 'child-attachment' behaviour emerged.

i Anxious avoidant.
  - 15 per cent of Ainsworth *et al*'s sample demonstrated this style.
  - On the whole they avoided the mother. They appeared to be indifferent to her presence.
  - They showed distress when left alone. However, a stranger could comfort them just as well as their mother.

ii Securely attached.
  - 70 per cent of Ainsworth *et al*'s sample demonstrated this style.
  - Children were happy and confident in mother's presence, and used her as a secure base from which to explore the environment.
  - They showed distress when left alone with a stranger and quickly went to her on her return.

iii Anxious resistant.
  - 15 per cent of Ainsworth *et al*'s sample demonstrated this style
  - Children had difficulties in using mother as a secure base.
  - They showed a need to be cuddled, but when the mother picked them up they struggled to get down. They demonstrated ambivalent emotions.

Conclusions: Children's attachment behaviours were classified into the above categories: 70 per cent of Ainsworth *et al*'s sample showed secure attachment, 15 per cent showed anxious-avoidant and 15 per cent showed anxious-resistant.

Commentary

The term 'secure base' is very useful in understanding how babies use their primary carer as a source of comfort and reassurance in times of distress, but also how it is used as a starting point from which to 'go off' and explore the world. Even though the work of Ainsworth looked at infant attachments, many psychologists have always stressed the importance of 'secure bonds' in relationships at any age. Bowlby (1977) suggested that 'attachment behaviour characterized humans from the cradle to the grave' and Weiss (1991) related attachments to the maintenance of emotional security in both children and adults. Freud believed that the 'mother-child' relationship was the 'prototype' of all later loving relationships, the inference being, if it was unsuccessful you were emotionally 'doomed for life'. It was Hazen and Shaver (1987) who first attempted to relate the concept of a 'secure base' to adult sexual relationships.

'Romantic love' and types of attachment

Hazen and Shaver (1987) proposed that adults use 'primitive' attachment styles in their later romantic relationships. These styles (or 'mental models') were internalized during childhood. They based these styles on Ainsworth *et al*'s 1978 classification. Participants were asked to respond to a newspaper 'Love Quiz', in which they were required to answer questions about their perceptions of romantic love (for a fuller account see Key Study 2).

As the conclusion to Hazen and Shaver's study suggests, it is not an inevitability that early attachments determine later ones. Main *et al* (1985) found that some adults had successfully managed to 'break free' from their own problematic attachments as children, and produce secure ones with their own children. Perhaps being aware of our own shortcomings helps us in not making the same mistakes with the next generation.

Attachment – the concept of 'babytalk'

Levels of attachment are often identified, through examining styles of communication. A mother will often use 'babytalk' in her interactions with her child. Babytalk is characterized by a melodious, high-pitched tone, in which carers convey sentiments of love and affection. Bombar and Littig (1996) propose that it is virtually universal among caretakers of infants and small children. However, babytalk also occurs between people where language development is not an issue. An example would include older adults in residential institutions (Caporael and Culbertson, 1986). Equally, it is not always interaction between humans where babytalk has been identified. Adults often use it when communicating with their pets (Levin and Hunter, 1982), or their favourite cuddly toy, even favourite plants. Bombar and Littig (1996) propose that despite the other benefits of babytalk (e.g. facilitation of language development), one of its primary functions is attachment:

'… it functions more generally in the process of mutual emotional connection, especially intimate psychological bonding, or secure attachment, and that it does so in a variety of relationships'(Bombar and Littig 1996).

Previous research has shown that couples often develop phrases or expressions (idioms) that are unique to them (e.g. Bruess and Pearson, 1993). It

KEY STUDY 2

Researchers:	Hazen and Shaver (1987)
Aims:	The main aim of this study was to explore the possibility that early childhood attachment patterns could influence later, adult romantic relationships.
Method:	Participants were asked to respond to a 'love quiz' in a local newspaper, which asked them firstly to identify the sort of relationship they had with their parents, and secondly to report their current feelings to romantic relationships. The correlations between these two questionnaires were assessed.
Results:	56 per cent of the participants were classified as securely attached. Features of this type of relationship included feeling comfortable about being dependent upon romantic partners.
	23–25 per cent of the participants were classified as anxious-avoidant. Features of this type of relationship included feeling uncomfortable when romantic partners got too close.
	19–20 per cent of the participants were classified as anxious-ambivalent. Features of this type of relationship included feeling worried that romantic partners didn't really love them.
Conclusions:	The research showed correlations between early attachment styles and later romantic ones. Even though the correlations were statistically significant they were not strong.

helps reinforce the 'special closeness' that exists between them. Furthermore studies have shown positive correlations between the number of idioms used by couples, their closeness and reported levels of love (Bell *et al*, 1987) and even levels of marital satisfaction (Bruess and Pearson, 1993).

Attachment – the 'cute concept'

As we have seen, all psychologists would agree to the importance of secure attachments in relationships, whatever the age. But what is it that 'draws us' closer to a person in the first place? Many researchers believe adults are 'programmed' to respond to certain features or 'cues' that facilitate interaction. Eibl-Eibesfeldt (1970) suggests that certain features of the human infant make us regard it as cuddly. He proposes the hallmarks of 'cuddliness' are:

'chubby cheeks; a forehead which is high and protruding in relation to the small face; relatively large eyes; a small mouth for sucking … and so on'.

In everyday terminology this is referred to as 'cute appeal'. Our brains are 'structured' in such a way that we respond positively to 'things' that are cute. We are programmed with a mental representation (a schema) of 'cuteness'. This idea was originally proposed by Lorenz (1943), in which he suggested that baby animals possess a 'cute appeal' that stimulates 'nurturing and caring behaviours' within adults. It certainly appears true that even the 'hardest' of adults can 'melt' at the sight of a beautiful baby or even a cuddly toy. However, it is not just babies who 'emanate' cute appeal, adults can maintain these features also. Perrett *et al* (1994) published a paper in *Nature*, which concluded that certain facial features (in adult females), predisposed them to be perceived as more attractive. What made this study more interesting was that it was cross-cultural, using Japanese participants also. The same facial features were perceived as attractive in both cultures (see Figure 1.4).

- High cheek bones
- Thin jaw
- Large eyes relative to size of face
- Short distance between mouth and chin
- Short distance between nose and mouth

Figure 1.4: Key features of the most attractive female face shape (taken from Perret et al, *1994).*

Commentary

Lorenz's ideas suggest that evolution has created a two-way relationship between cuteness and caring:
- The individual (be it a child or adult) who possesses more 'cute features' will elicit more caring and nurturing behaviour from a 'significant' adult.

- The adult, on the other hand, must respond with caring and nurturing behaviour on exposure to 'cute features'. Even though these ideas may appear to possess a simplistic charm, further issues remain. Firstly, what happens to those individuals who lack 'cuteness' in terms of their physical appearance? Also what happens to adults who appear not to respond with caring or nurturing when presented with 'cute people or things'? Evolutionary theorists would no doubt respond by suggesting that these people were dysfunctional and therefore less likely to survive and reproduce!

It appears that many psychologists are in agreement that certain features are perceived as cute, but at what age do we start responding to 'cute signals' in a caring and nurturing way (see RLA 3)?

Summary

- It has always been assumed that babies show 'nurturing behaviour' from birth.
- Morris *et al* (1996) have shown that younger babies prefer to be nurtured themselves. It isn't until about 4–6 years old, that children start responding in a nurturant way to 'baby-like' objects.
- Results such as these suggest that it is adults that maintain and shape the multi-million-pound cuddly toy industry.

Questions

1 In your own words summarize the key findings of Morris *et al*'s study.

2 Do these results regarding 'nurturing behaviour' make sense from an evolutionary perspective?

Attachment – physical contact

The sense of touch is one of our most primitive behaviours. It shouldn't be too surprising therefore to find it as a fundamental part of relationships. For most of us, our earliest experience was cuddling (or as some psychologists refer to it as 'contact comfort') usually from our mother, or another primary caregiver. Indeed some studies have shown (e.g. Kaitz *et al*, 1992) that it is possible for mothers to recognize their offspring by touch alone.

New-borns (neonates) show a range of behaviours that encourage touch by their carers. In the previous section we looked at 'cute appeal'. In most cases

Real Life Application 3:
The evolution of cuddly toys

A widely held belief assumes that nurturing responses are present in babyhood. We assume babies want to cuddle 'soft toys', that is why they are bought them. Paul Morris and colleagues from the Department of Psychology at the University of Portsmouth, set up a study to determine at what age children begin to engage in nurturing behaviour. They used four 'baby-faced teddies' and four 'adult-featured bears', and showed them to three groups of children: 4-year-olds, 6-year-olds and 8-year-olds. Out of the younger children, 17 out of the 24 preferred the 'adult-featured bears', but in the older ages significant preference was showed to the 'baby-faced bears'. As Morris *et al* conclude:

'... babies prefer what would give them nurture, rather than the other way around'.

They go on to suggest that adults buy children cute cuddly toys, based upon their own (adult) perceptions of cuteness. It appears that the multi-million-pound, cuddly toy market is 'driven' by adults for adults!

Article adapted from 'Bear facts reveal the truth behind teddies' by Nigel Hawkes, *The Times*, 27 January 1996.

Real Life Application 4:
Primitive relationships – the 'power of touch'

Material A – bonding
In 1959, Harlow and Zimmerman carried out a series of experiments using baby rhesus monkeys. They separated the babies shortly after birth and placed them in cage with two 'surrogate mothers'. One of these mothers consisted of a wire frame, the other a wire frame covered in soft cloth. The baby monkeys spent significantly more time cuddling the cloth surrogate than the wire, and this finding persisted even when a milk bottle was attached to the 'wire mother' (see Figure 1.5). It appeared that 'cuddling' was preferable to feeding. It was also found that when the babies were distressed (which was induced by presenting a noisy toy into the monkeys' cage), they showed a significant preference for the 'soft surrogate' mothers. The researchers concluded that bonding appears to be most effective when there is 'contact comfort'.

Material B – Premature babies
Until the late 1970s, babies who had been born prematurely were touched as little as possible for fear of infection. Mothers and fathers watched

Figure 1.5: A rhesus monkey experiencing contact comfort.

babies have to do very little apart from lying back and looking cute. They are relying on adults possessing the 'schema' that stimulates caring and nurturing behaviours. However, babies don't just rely on their 'naturally appealing looks'. Smiling is probably one of the most captivating and irresistible of all infant behaviours. Studies have shown that by three months the sight of the baby's primary care-giver (usually the mother) initiates the smiling response (Adamson and Bakeman, 1985). The 'social smile' encourages carers to interact with their offspring.

Touch – a primitive relationship
A number of studies have looked at the importance of touch from its evolutionary perspective. There is little doubt touch is a 'primitive behaviour', and therefore has a deep and powerful significance. During the late 1950s and early 1960s, a series of studies was conducted by Harlow and colleagues which confirmed the importance of 'physical contact'. More recently, scientists have been able to apply these ideas to the care of premature babies (see RLA 4).

from a distance as their precious child lay, connected to a whole host of medical paraphernalia. Today, however opinions have changed, thanks to pioneering research (partly influenced by Harlow's work), by investigators such as Saul Schanberg and Tiffany Field. Schanberg *et al* (1990) found that removing rat pups (babies) from their mothers, decreased levels of an enzyme responsible for normal growth. If he artificially simulated the mothers' 'licking behaviour' by stroking them with a small paintbrush, the enzyme returned to normal levels. They concluded:

'the need for a mother's touch is really brain based. It isn't just nice to have it. It is a requirement for the normal development and growth of the baby'.

Continuing with this work, Field and Schanberg (1990) set up a study to look at the effects of massaging premature human infants, while in special care baby units. They found that babies who had been massaged gained more weight, and were able to go home sooner, compared to the non-massaged neonates. What is possibly more surprising is that eight months later, the weight advantage had remained, and also the massaged infants showed more advanced cognitive, motor and emotional development (Field 1990).

Article from *Advances in touch*, 1990.

Summary

- Harlow demonstrated that 'contact comfort' was of fundamental importance to neonate monkeys.
- Schanberg *et al*'s work illustrated that there is a link between 'touch' and physiological systems.
- Today, it is seen as good paediatric practice to encourage parents to cuddle their premature babies as much as possible. Studies such as Field and Schanberg's (1990) highlight the benefits.

Questions

1 How do Harlow's findings relate to Maslow's Hierarchy of Needs, as discussed in Section 1 (see p. 3)?

2 Summarize some of the evolutionary benefits of 'touch'.

3 What is the mind designed to do?

As we are beginning to see, engaging in relationships provides many benefits for us. In evolutionary terms this makes perfect sense. Two very specific benefits will be briefly considered now. These are:

- sexual reproduction (mating strategies)
- improved immune system functioning.

Mating strategies

Evolution has designed humans to reproduce. This is a highly effective method of allowing genes to continue. However, it would be more beneficial if reproduction followed certain rules or patterns, to maximize reproductive success. That is exactly what evolutionists argue has emerged. They refer to these as 'mating strategies'. Evolutionary theory suggests that men and women differ in the types of strategies they adopt.

Commentary

Evidence that there are sex differences in mating strategies comes from a rather 'dubious', but very simple survey conducted by Clarke and Hatfield (1989). They used an attractive person (of the opposite sex) to ask American college students if they would like to have sex with them! 100 per cent of the women in the survey refused whereas 75 per cent of the men agreed.

Men, it appears are more receptive to casual sex than women. One explanation for this is that men cannot be certain that they are the parent of potential offspring, whereas a mother can (by the fact she gave birth to the child).

Paternity uncertainty

As has just been pointed out, one of the major problems which faced our male human ancestors was paternity uncertainty (not knowing if they were the father). It has only been in the last ten years or so that advances in genetic testing have allowed us to confirm paternity. Some evolutionary theorists argue that marriage provided one solution to this problem (Strassman, 1981). Another solution would be to identify those females who have had no previous sexual contact (pre-marital chastity). Clearly, this would have been extremely difficult. However, contemporary studies do indicate that men more than women appear to emphasize chastity as being important in the choice of a long-term mate. Buss and Schmitt (1993) found that in a cross-cultural study of attitudes towards chastity, participants from China, India and Palestinian Arab areas of Israel viewed virginity as important, whereas participants from Sweden, Norway, West Germany and France did not.

Commentary

Findings such as these suggest attitudes towards chastity aren't so much influenced by our evolution, but by the 'social norms' of different cultures.

If our male ancestors could not be sure that they were the father of any offspring, and they couldn't be sure that their sexual partner was a virgin, the final solution would have been clear. Have sexual relationships with as many females as possible, as this increases the chances of paternity. Male promiscuity has an evolutionary pedigree (Moir and Jessel, 1989). But what of females? What is their mating imperative?

Female strategies

Evolutionary theory has always stressed that females' primary imperative is to produce offspring, and to provide nurture, until the child is capable of looking after itself. Women therefore tend to be more cautious when choosing a potential mate, because they have to assess their protective qualities (Trivers, 1979).

Commentary

A good way of understanding the evolutionary differences between male and female mating strategies, is summarized in what became known as the 'Coolidge effect' (Symons 1979).

The US President and his wife were visiting a farm. As they passed the chicken pens, Mrs Coolidge enquired how often the rooster copulated each day:

'Dozens of times was the reply. Please tell that to the president, Mrs Coolidge requested. When the president passed the pens and was told about the rooster, he asked, same hen every time? Oh no, Mr President, a different one each time. The president nodded slowly, then said, Tell that to Mrs Coolidge …'

We must remember, however, as we have already seen, evolution can be 'overwritten' by social and cultural factors.

Improved immune system functioning

Paul Martin (1997) makes the point:

'*Evolution has equipped our bodies with psychological and biological mechanisms which enable the brain and immune system to talk to each other.*'

The research literature is full of studies that suggest social relationships are good for our immune systems. For example, Kiecolt-Glaser (1993) found that women whose marriages had broken down within the previous year had impaired immune functioning compared to married women. The women who suffered the worst 'immune suppression' were those who retained high emotional attachment to the ex-partners.

Commentary

Another study, conducted by Coe *et al*, showed the biological effects of separating baby monkeys from their mothers. They found that initially the babies showed outward signs of stress, and that these correlated with impaired immune functioning. But after a while, the outward behavioural signs of stress diminished. However, stress hormone levels continued to rise, signifying potential damage to the immune system. This finding shows that outward behaviour can give a misleading impression of what's going on inside the body.

4 How does our current environment affect our primitively developed mind?

There are many ways in which our 'evolutionary behavioural legacy' affects contemporary society. However, this legacy is not always as useful as it used to be. There are some commentators who believe we are not well suited to our current environment (e.g. James, 1998). As Buss (1999) points out, our ancestors lived in small groups, making relationships more simplistic. Today, we are exposed to potentially millions of people and multi-media images of 'perfect humans'. One contemporary area that has been looked at using an evolutionary framework is infidelity. A recent study by Pento-Voak (1999) implies that women may be just as promiscuous as males, and that it is in their evolutionary interests to be so (see Real Life Application 5).

Summary

- Pento-Voak's (1999) work suggests that women could be 'programmed' to have affairs, to benefit their genetic line.
- It has only been in the last decade or so that DNA testing has allowed scientists to determine paternity.
- Studies show that the incidence of wrongful paternity could be as high as one in six.

Real Life Application 5:

The evolution of infidelity

Material A

A controversial theory has emerged giving weight to the idea that infidelity could have evolutionary advantages. Ian Pento-Voak (1999) of St Andrews University and researchers at the University of Tokyo observed that female participants found different men's faces sexually attractive, based on where they were in their menstrual cycle. Prior to and immediately after menstruation (a period), when a woman is less likely to conceive, their participants found 'softer' more feminine features preferable. During the middle part of the menstrual cycle (when it is more likely that conception will occur), their participants found 'harder' more 'rugged masculine' features attractive.

The researchers made the following conclusions. More masculine features such as a 'strong jaw' and larger nose could be an indication of increased fertility and good overall health in males. A 'softer' more delicate profile of facial features could indicate a 'weaker' genetic predisposition, however signify a more kind and caring personality. Evolution has perhaps programmed women to be attracted to more 'rugged', genetically stronger men when they are most likely to conceive. In the words of the researchers:

'A female might choose a primary partner whose low masculine appearance suggests co-operation in parental care … but occasionally copulate with a male with a more masculine appearance.'

They go on to suggest, unlike mothers (who give birth to their offspring), fathers cannot be certain of their paternity. For this reason women could have benefited from a mixed mating strategy – or to put it another way having affairs.

Article adapted from *Nature*, 399, 24 June 1999.

Material B
Paternity testing

A technique known as 'genetic fingerprinting' is used to test for familial relationships. It involves using a radio-labelled probe to examine a highly variable region of the DNA of the genome. The unique pattern this produces is related to the patterns shown by the individual's parents. Through this scientists are able to identify a child's father in paternity disputes.

Material C
'Wrongful paternity'

An article published in the *Journal of the American Medical Association* by Sussman and Schatkin (1995) found that 12 out of 67 expectant fathers who voluntarily submitted to blood tests, who had previously believed themselves to be the fathers, were more than likely not. This equates to one in six!

Adapted from *Journal of American Medical Association*, 164/3, p. 249.

Questions

1 In what ways do Pento-Voak's (1999) findings contradict what you have already read about sex differences in evolutionary explanations of mating strategies?

2 What does the information in Material C tell you about women's mating strategies in contemporary society?

All the theories and ideas we have looked at so far come from an evolutionary or biological perspective. However, there are many commentators on relationships who propose more psychological and social explanations of why humans need other people. We will start by considering balance theory.

Balance theory of relationships

Balance theory was originally developed by Heider (1958). He proposed a simple system which described the way in which people perceive the world. It involved three factors: **1** the person (P), **2** another person (O), and **3** an object (X) which could also be a third person. According to balance theory P, O and X can be related in terms of values. Dislike is represented by a −, whereas liking is represented by a +. In order to make sense of the model let us look at an example. Imagine that Peter (P) likes Oriella (O). Oriella also likes Peter. However, she doesn't like football (X), which Peter does. This could be represented by the following triad:

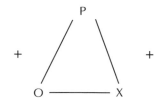

Clearly, this situation is not in balance. According to Heider (1958), something has to change. According to Rosenberg and Abelson (1960), attitudes change according to a principle of 'minimum effort'. In this example that would probably mean that Oriella would have to develop a positive attitude towards football. The triad would then look like this:

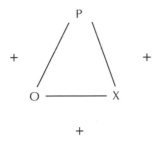

Heider (1958) proposed a possible eight triad situations (see Figure 1.6): in the diagram a–d are balanced, e–h are not, and would therefore require attitude changes.

Commentary

Heider's ideas perhaps fit in well with our intuitive views on relationships. However, there are problems. Firstly, where X is a third person, the theory suggests solutions that are too simplistic in real life. For example, if Peter (P) likes Oriella (O) and Oriella likes Mike (X) and Peter dislikes Mike the following triad would be created:

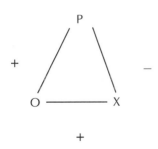

It would be inconceivable to believe that the solution to this 'love triad' would be solved by everyone liking each other (see below), and thereby creating balance as Heider suggests:

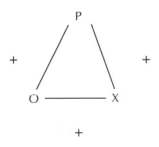

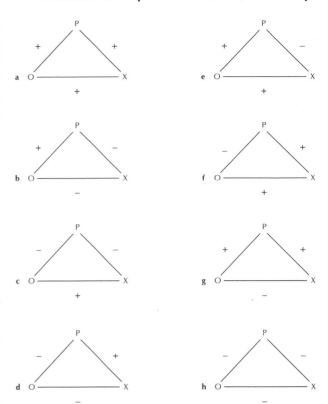

Figure 1.6: Heider's (1958) eight triad situations

The following would appear to be the more logical solution, where Peter would be forced to 'go off' Oriella:

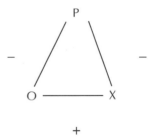

Secondly, another problem with balance theory is that the values are only assessed in terms of like or dislike. No indication is given as to the intensity of the feeling. Thirdly, it doesn't take into account more complicated interactions. It only deals with relationships between three entities.

Newcombe (1971) reformulated Heider's original ideas, and applied them directly to interpersonal attraction. One of the important features of Newcombe's ideas was his suggestion that three states existed between the three entities (P, O and X), namely balance, imbalance and non-balance. If you recall Heider had suggested just the two, balance and imbalance. For Newcombe, balanced situations

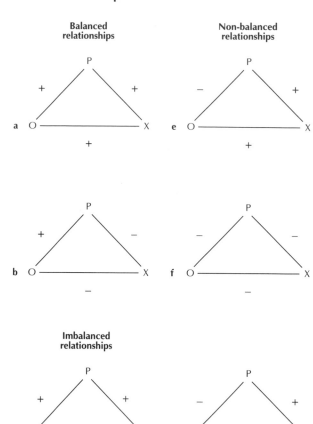

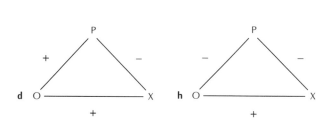

Balance: Peter (P) likes Oriella (O) and she likes Mike (X). Peter also likes Mike. This scenario might explain why it is possible to judge a person by analysing their friends.

Imbalance: Peter (P) likes Oriella (O), however she doesn't like Mike (X). Peter likes Mike. There are a number of ways in which this imbalance can be resolved:
• Peter can stop liking Oriella.
• Peter can stop liking Mike.
• Oriella can begin to like Mike.

Non-balance: Peter (P) likes Mike (X), however Mike doesn't like Oriella (O). Peter likes Oriella. Because Peter doesn't mind that Mike and Oriella don't get on, there is little motivation to change the situation. There isn't balance, however it isn't perceived as a problem.

Figure 1.7: Newcombe's reformulation of Heider's theory, showing balanced, non-balanced and imbalanced relationships.

created pleasant feelings for the participants and there is no need for change. Imbalance situations created unpleasant feelings and there was a strong need for change. Non-balance, according to Newcombe, was where disagreement occurred between the participants. However, the differences of opinion were not perceived to be important (there was indifference). In this situation there was little motivation to want to change. Figure 1.7 summarizes Newcombe's categories, and gives three life examples.

There are a number of studies which appear to support balance theory. Curtis and Miller (1986) proposed that we are attracted to those who we believe are attracted to us. Also we don't expect our friends and enemies to get along (Chapdelaine, 1994). It is also suggested that we like those people who are friends with our existing friends, and dislike those who are friends with our enemies (Aronson and Cope, 1986). This could explain why many successful relationships start off as introductions from friends.

Relationships explained by learning theory

Reinforcement

Operant conditioning is based upon the concept of reinforcement and was developed by Skinner (1904–90). He proposed (through his version of the 'law of effect') that **positive reinforcement** strengthens behaviours, whereas **punishment** weakens them. Through his work with laboratory rats and pigeons, he found that the animals would actively engage in behaviours which produced a 'positive outcome' (namely a food pellet). In the case of rats this behaviour involved pressing a lever as a means of delivering the food. If the outcome of lever-pressing resulted in an electric shock (punishment) the behaviour quickly ceased. This theory suggests that behaviours (and their associated emotions) are more likely to be repeated if the individual associates a 'positive experience' (reward) with them. Often that experience can influence how we perceive other people. Imagine you were out on a first date in a romantic candlelit restaurant. Soft music was playing and the person you were with was making you laugh a lot and taking a genuine interest in you as an individual. The interaction would be full of positive reinforcement, therefore you will associate the person with a great evening (see Figure 1.8). Byrne and Clore (1970) claimed that it is important that we are aware of the rewards and punishments that other

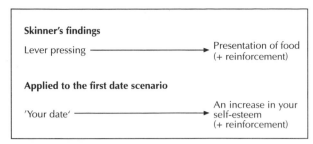

Figure 1.8: The concept of positive reinforcement

people provide, as we use these as a good estimation of how successful a relationship will be.

Commentary

An early study conducted by Lott and Lott (1968) attempted to illustrate this point. They observed children's relationships with one another after they had experienced rewarding or punishing classroom environments. They found that children who had received consistent rewards from their teachers showed a higher level of liking for their fellow classmates than those who experienced a punishing regime. It appeared that the classroom atmosphere created by the teacher affected the quality of the inter-personal relationships of the pupils. A more recent example was conducted by May and Hamilton (1980). They asked female participants to rate male photographs in three conditions: firstly, while pleasant background music was playing, secondly while 'unpleasant' music played and thirdly with no music at all (the control condition). They found that those females who were exposed to the pleasant music rated the men as better looking, when compared with the other conditions.

Clearly, the previous paragraph stresses the importance of thought and emotion as an accompaniment to behaviour. Humans rarely behave outside of an emotional context. The example given of a first date illustrates how our interpretation of others can become associated with a number of factors, in this case all positive. However, the evening could have gone horribly wrong, leaving you feeling hurt and belittled. The date would have been equivalent to 'punishment' and therefore (according to Skinner's theory) reduced the likelihood of you going out with that person again.

Further examples of punishment

Just as some factors can be rewarding, others can have the opposite effect. Often we develop powerful pre-conceived ideas about someone based on very tenuous knowledge. If you happen to meet an individual who resembles someone you knew in the past, perhaps at school, and who you disliked, this unfortunate person can often be 'tarred with the same brush'. Names are an excellent example of this. If we have had a 'bad' experience with a person in the past, his or her name would become associated with unpleasant memories. In future interactions, initially, we may be wary of someone of that name. Unfamiliarity of a name has been shown to have similar effects. Colman *et al* (1981) found that first names that were rated as highly familiar (such as David) created more initial liking than less familiar names (such as Fulbert). These created initial negative perceptions.

Commentary

'Bad' relationship experiences in the past can make us wary of certain looks or mannerisms and even names. Also studies such as Colman's suggest that names that we are not familiar with are perceived in a more unfavourable light. What we 'take into' a potential relationship (our past emotional associations) can clearly influence its progression.

Over the years psychologists have interested themselves in what factors constitute positive reinforcement or rewards. Let us now consider some.

Holding similar attitudes

Byrne and Nelson (1965) demonstrated that the more a couple share in common (in terms of their attitudes and beliefs) the higher their reported attraction for one another. The fact that two people 'have things in common' acts as positive reinforcement. Rubins (1973) believes this is because holding similar attitudes strengthens our self-esteem. We know that someone else agrees with us, therefore making our views appear more valid. Also sharing common ground allows us to interact with others in a more productive and meaningful way. More can be achieved because we are moving in the same direction and share common goals.

Reciprocity

It is very difficult to dislike someone if you are aware they genuinely like you. In terms of popularity it shouldn't be too surprising to find that individuals who engage in 'rewarding behaviours' are the most liked (Argyle,1992). Often we feel almost obliged to like them because they like us. So how does reciprocity come about? Does an individual hear that he or she is liked, then **reciprocate** that liking, or do we like someone, then assume that the person will like us. Backman and Secord (1959) conducted a study in which complete strangers were asked to talk with one another. Certain individuals had been told 'up front' that certain other members of the group would like them. It was found that by about the second 'group session' participants preferred most those individuals they had been told would like them. However, as the sessions went on, by the sixth meeting, participants preferred most those individuals who genuinely appeared to like them, rather than those they had been told 'up front' would like them.

Commentary

A further study conducted in 1965 by Aronson and Linder again illustrated that reciprocity isn't quite as straightforward as it might appear. They found that participants develop the strongest attraction for one another when they 'start off' negative at first, then become much warmer. Often this 'concept' is used in Hollywood films between heroes and heroines. They begin the film arguing and fighting, but end up falling 'madly in love'.

Materialistic reinforcement

Often individuals find themselves 'drawn' to other people purely and simply because they can 'provide' for them in materialistic ways. Homans (1974) proposed that one of the most powerful reinforcers is 'social approval'. Because Western culture values aesthetics (looks), status and power, being with someone who can provide some of these is often seen as desirable. One of the richest men in the world is Yoshiaki Tsutsumi, a Japanese businessman in his late sixties. He has been linked with many relationships, particularly to young and beautiful actresses. According to his close friends he supports a number of households, each with a wife and children. His wealth has been estimated at over US$22 billion. From the opposite perspective Elder (1969) argued that beautiful women have an advantage in attracting highly successful mates.

Commentary

Goodwin (1999) attempts to explain why some cultures place great importance on individuality (looking after yourself) and others on collectiveness (looking after the community as a whole). One reason he proposes is that the more wealthy cultures are able to think in individualistic ways because they have the resources to do so. Clearly, Yoshiaki Tsutsumi's 'individualistic' acquisition of wealth has given him status and power. A final point

regarding 'reinforcement theories' is that not only do they stress individualism (as we have just seen) but they also assume that everyone only thinks about their own 'positive reinforcement' within relationships. Often, however, people focus on what they can provide for others.

'Positive strokes'

Eric Berne (1964) in his classic book *Games people play* uses the term 'stroking' to identify behaviours that acknowledge another's presence. These could include kind words, compliments or a literal 'pat on the back'. He proposed we all need 'positive' strokes as these are vital for our well-being.

The economic theories of relationships

A third major group of explanations is commonly referred to as the economic theories. They are similar to learning theories in so much as they stress the importance of certain behaviours acting as reinforcement. However, one of the major differences is that, unlike 'reinforcement' theories, economic theories consider the relative values people place on specific attributes. We mentioned earlier that possessions and wealth can be reinforcing, but that is dependent upon how much an individual values these commodities. Economic theories stress the interaction of values between people.

Social exchange theory

This idea was originally put forward by Thibaut and Kelley in 1959. It proposed that people assess their relationships in terms of costs and benefits (rewards). They argued that we can predict how successful a relationship will be if we know two factors:

1 the level of rewards an individual gains from being in a relationship with another
2 what level of rewards an individual believes he or she should receive from being in a relationship with another (the so-called comparison level).

Commentary

Point 1 is relatively straightforward. If a person feels that his or her relationship fulfils important needs in his or her life, then he or she will appraise it in a positive way. If, on the other hand, important needs are unfulfilled, it will be appraised in a negative light. Point 2 suggests that individuals 'go into' relationships expecting certain things. Thibaut and Kelley (1959) argue that these expectations will be based upon previous relationships. However, some commentators believe that social exchange theory needs to incorporate some 'notion of general expectations', which could be obtained from a wider variety of sources (Pennington, 1986). We could, for example, assess our own relationships in terms of media influences, work colleagues or close friends relationships. Our friends may have qualities in their relationships that we admire and wish for ourselves. How often have you heard friends saying to each other 'I wish I had a relationship with my boyfriend/girlfriend like yours'.

Another major feature of social exchange theory was its development of an explanatory model. It can be used in a variety of relationship settings, apart from romantic ones. For example, a relationship between an employee and his or her boss will not last very long if the employee feels that he or she is investing more than is being received; it is likely the employee will look for another job. Indeed, research has found that, when rewards are available in alternative relationships, an individual will be less committed to stay in his or her current relationship situation (Drigotas and Rusbult, 1992). However, if people are already committed and investing heavily in a relationship, they are less likely to look actively for alternatives (Simpson *et al*, 1990).

Equity theory

One of the key proponents of equity theory was Homans (1974). He developed the ideas of social exchange theory by suggesting that successful relationships need to be in harmony and balance (equity). In real life this means that we need to get out of a relationship roughly the same amount as we put into it. A basic formula for this would be:

$$\frac{\text{Person A}}{\text{Contributions}} \; \text{Benefits} = \frac{\text{Person B}}{\text{Contributions}} \; \text{Benefits}$$

This is fine if everything is in balance, but what would happen if there is inequality within a relationship? One solution was identified by Elaine Walster (1978), who tested the notion that if marriage partners did not feel that they were getting equal amounts out of a relationship, they would attempt to resolve this imbalance by engaging in extra-marital affairs. She found this hypothesis to be the case. Those who felt 'hard done by' engaged in extra-marital sex earlier in their marriages and had more extra-marital partners than their more equitable counterparts.

Commentary

More recently, Van Yperen and Buunk (1990) carried out a study using 736 married couples and found that 'feeling equity' for wives predicted 'marital satisfaction'. However, this effect was much weaker for the husbands. Perhaps one explanation to this finding is that on the whole men are poor at assessing relationships. Indeed, Burnett (1986) suggests that men have less understanding of relationships than women.

Is equity theory really as straightforward as it might appear? Arguably, it is not the equality in terms of amount (quantity), but equality in terms of the significance to the individual (quality). Your need to be with a highly attractive person could be so strong (perhaps due to some deep-seated insecurity) that you would be quite happy to sacrifice intelligent conversation and long-term commitment to achieve this benefit. The benefit to you in this example outweighs the costs. However, this situation would not suit all individuals.

Commentary

One question that has been asked regarding equity theory is, 'Do we really go to all that trouble to "cognitively assess" the balance of all our relationships?'. Cate and Lloyd (1988) suggested that we perhaps take a more general overview of 'what we get out' than create some sort of exact score. If our impression is we receive a significant number of good things, then our overall view of that relationship will be positive. On a rather cynical note, Blau (1968) suggests 'people end up with the mates they deserve'.

Essay questions

1 Outline and evaluate explanations of why humans engage in relationships.

2 Discuss psychological explanations of the process of affiliations (AEB, Summer 1994).

3 What are the problems associated with using an 'evolutionary framework' when explaining relationships?

The development of relationships

This chapter looks at how relationships develop, from initial attraction through to long-term stability or ultimate breakdown. It starts by looking at factors which influence attraction, namely prior expectations, physical looks, similarity, complementarity, familiarity and fallibility. It then goes on to consider the effects of non-verbal communication (NVC) and self disclosure. The second part of the chapter looks at theories as to why relationships keep going. The last area focuses upon the breakdown of relationships, and in particular considers adultery, jealousy and divorce. Real Life Applications that are considered are:

- RLA 6: The face of beauty
- RLA 7: Finding a partner in the personal ads
- RLA 8: Jealousy – a pathological condition?

Attraction

We have all experienced it before. You see someone at a 'social gathering' and immediately you decide you would like to get to know that person better. Attraction can take many forms. An individual could be attracted to someone because he or she finds the person sexually appealing (as in the case of models or film stars). It could be because the other person intrigues or fascinates them (as in the case of enigmatic leaders). Admiration could be the trigger (as any person knows who has ever been a fan of a pop or sports star). Whoever the initial attraction is aimed at, it is always based upon very limited information. Initially, we know nothing about the person, so what is our initial 'picture' based upon? Scientists have identified two factors: expectations and physical looks. We will consider these in turn.

Expectations

Sometimes we get to know a little about the background of an individual before we have actually met the person. Friends pass on information or may talk about people: 'See that man over there, he's a dentist'. Even if we have no information at all, humans appear to have a 'knack' of forming an immediate impression. This isn't a new phenomenon. The mathematician Pythagoras (500 BC) used to assess the mathematical prowess of his students by 'look-

ing into their eyes'. Hippocrates (the founding father of modern medicine) used to make instantaneous judgements regarding his patients' health, by looking at them for a few seconds.

Commentary

Humans readily judge other people, and create a 'snap shot' opinion of them. This either helps to create initial attraction, or not. Studies have shown it isn't just people that we can be instantly attracted to. Products, places, even 'nonsense concepts' can create immediate reactions. Goleman (1995) found that English-speaking participants showed more of a preference for the nonsense word 'juvalamu' than 'chakaka'. This has obvious relevance when marketers are creating names for new products.

Over the years there have been many attempts to explain how expectations are formed. We will consider two ideas, the fundamental attribution error and the self-fulfilling prophecy.

The fundamental attribution error

A classic psychological principle states that people tend to overestimate the role of personal characteristics and minimize the social setting when explaining the behaviour of others. This has become known as the fundamental attribution error (Ross, 1977). If we were to see someone arrive at a party driving an expensive sports car, it is likely we would perceive the person as being successful and wealthy (i.e. the individual is credited with the success). An equally viable, but not as common explanation could be the car was being delivered to a client by an 'averagely successful' car sales rep.

Commentary

Arguably there are two possible explanations for the fundamental attribution error. Heider (1958) suggested that people are more likely to make attributions to things which are salient (stand out). Therefore, when we see someone at a 'social gathering' it is the person our attention focuses on, not the situation or setting. The second explanation suggests that it is Western culture that perpetuates this error. Westerners on the whole are brought up to value autonomy and independence as desirable characteristics. Therefore, it isn't difficult to see why attributions made by Westerners tend to focus on the person. In non-Western cultures where individualism is not so valued, the fundamental attribution error is less apparent. Morris and Peng (1994) found that American and Chinese students showed no difference in their attributions for physical events, but Americans showed a preference for personal attributions for social events.

The self-fulfilling prophecy

Rosenthal and Jacobson (1968) published a paper entitled *Pygmalion in the classroom*. In it they demonstrated that if teachers' expectations of children were positive (regardless of the pupils' actual ability) they performed better. If the teachers had initially created poorer expectations, those children performed worse. It was the teachers' expectations of how well the pupils would do that appeared to shape the pupils' actual behaviour. Figure 2.1 illustrates how this process may occur.

Commentary

So initial judgements of people can be influenced by attributing characteristics to the person rather than the situation, and by individuals' responses towards other people. In fact, being continually responded to in a particular way can create a 'biased self image' which can have a direct effect on our social interactions. An ingenious study was set up to investigate exactly this. It has been well documented in a number of studies that people who are overweight are perceived as less attractive (e.g. Harris *et al* 1982). Miller *et al* (1990) allowed students to converse with either obese or non-obese women over the telephone (so that the women could not actually be seen). They found that despite the students

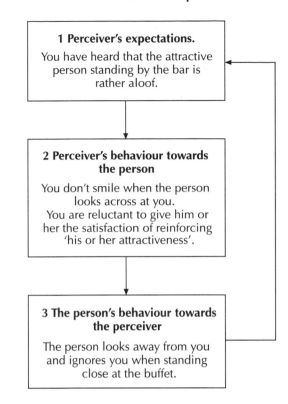

Figure 2.1: Imagine you are the perceiver

having no idea about the women's appearance or size the non-obese women were rated as more attractive and socially skilled. One explanation for these findings was that the obese women were not as 'positive' or appealing in their voices as the non-obese. This could be due to a lack of confidence created over many years of feeling 'unattractive'.

As mentioned at the beginning of this chapter, assessments of attractiveness are based upon prior expectations and looks. We can form an impression of someone based upon information we receive before meeting them. Often, the prior expectations and appearance are processed simultaneously, and judgements have to be amended. Meeting someone you have heard over the telephone or on the radio is a good example of this. We create an image of a person based upon what he or she says, the sound of his or her voice. When we actually meet the person he or she looks nothing like we had imagined. Sometimes this can be pleasantly surprising, at other times it can be downright disappointing. We will now look at some of the factors that affect physical looks.

Physical looks

There is no doubt about it, physical appearance is the number one factor when it comes to attraction.

Research into this field can be divided into two distinct areas of investigation. Firstly, studies look at how we define what is attractive or beautiful and how perceptions of attraction and beauty change over time and between cultures. As will be seen shortly, much of this work has now been coveted by science. Secondly, research looks at what effects attractive people have on others. We will now consider both these in turn.

Definitions of attraction and beauty

Defining what is beautiful is possibly the most subjective behaviour a human can experience. The *Oxford English Dictionary* defines beauty as:

'*... a combination of qualities that give pleasure to the sight or other senses or to the mind*'.

Anthropologist Don Symons takes a very evolutionary and biological view of beauty by suggesting

'*... beauty is not so much in the eye as in the brain circuitry of the beholder*'.

In Western culture beauty is a multi-million-pound industry, and glamour models play a vital role in defining 'what is beautiful'. Maria Castagne, a director of Elite Model Management (a 'top' international model agency), suggests:

'*Judgements of beauty are instinctual not scientific. It is luck if a girl makes it. If a designer/photographer likes her/uses her she will become big.*'

Clearly, a young girl must have a certain 'aesthetic appeal' to have been considered by an agency in the first place. However, beauty can even transcend the aesthetic value placed on someone. Having met the English novelist George Eliot, Henry James wrote:

'*She is magnificently ugly. She has a low forehead, a dull grey eye, a vast pendulous nose, a huge mouth full of uneven teeth ... Now in this vast ugliness resides a most powerful beauty which, in a very few minutes, steals forth and charms the mind, so that you end as I ended, in falling in love with her.*'

A history of female beauty

Throughout history art has provided a commentary on what humans find beautiful. There have been a number of representations found within prehistoric art of the female body. These images are referred to as the 'prehistoric Venuses'. The most celebrated of these is known as the Venus of Laussel (see Figure 2.2). As can be seen, she possesses large hips and

Figure 2.2: The Venus of Laussel

breasts, which academics interpret as symbols of fertility. The small delicate hand is placed on the belly, again perhaps indicating links to childbirth.

This theme is seen again in India in the second century. Figure 2.3 portrays Yakshini (the tree goddess), with her slim waist, wide hips and full bust. It again illustrates the ideal of female beauty existing in India in this period.

In fifteenth-century Europe very little changed. The Flemish artist Rubens depicted beautiful women with 'rolls of fat' and ample breasts. During the Victorian period, the female body was required to be covered. Exposure of wrists, arms and legs were forbidden, even table and piano legs were draped with clothes, lest they aroused the passions of young gentlemen! Ironically, attempts were made to accentuate what was hidden under clothes. The Victorian bustle (an elaborate decoration attached to the bottom) exaggerated the buttocks.

In the post-war 1920s women's fashion became more revealing and awareness of the more 'rounded' female figure once again became 'in vogue'. One of the major influences on beauty at this time was the 'newly emerging' media. The early years of film pro-

Figure 2.3: The tree goddess, Yakshini

duced heroines such as Mae West and Jane Russell. Again large breasts and wide-childbearing hips were perceived as attractive. Arguably this image reached its peak during the 1950s with Marilyn Monroe. The 'busty blonde bombshell' image took on cult status, and it is still emulated today. However, the 1960s heralded a major change in the portrayal of the female body. Fashion models such as Twiggy led a trend that changed Western attitudes. She was very slender, had thin hips and a flat chest. More and more fashion photographers started working with young girls that fitted this description. The 1960s marked the beginning of the 'slim female look'. This was taken to an extreme in the 1990s with models such as Kate Moss, whose figure popularized the 'waif look', an ultra-thin appearance.

More recently, an article appeared in the magazine *Marie Claire* (June 2000) identifying a trend in Hollywood actresses for severe weight loss. The article dubbed actresses such as Calista Flockhart and Portia de Rossi as 'lollipop ladies', due to their 'stick-like bodies and seemly oversized heads'. Ironically, the same article points out that there isn't the same pressure on male actors to look thin. One Hollywood commentator pointed out:

'Men can hide their imperfections more easily – women's bodies are totally subject to the whims of the industry.'

Commentary

For the past 8000 years of human development, regardless of culture, women have been portrayed primarily as having large breasts and hips. Scientists subscribing to an evolutionary perspective (such as Singh, 1993 – see p. 10) would argue this is appealing to men because it signals fertility and reproductive success. But how have men been portrayed over time, and what has research shown, regarding 'male beauty'?

Male beauty

The Ancient Greeks frequently portrayed the male figure in marble statues. They were muscular, and well proportioned. Evolutionists attribute a muscular frame with strength and power, providing our male ancestors with youthful athleticism, to run and hunt across the ancient savannah. But how important is this ancient legacy in male beauty in the modern world?

Contemporary research into male beauty

As was mentioned in Chapter 1 (p. 7), a major survey into male appearance was conducted in the November/December 1993 edition of *Psychology Today*, a popular American magazine. Over 1500 readers responded. Sixty-four per cent were women. The average age for the female respondents was 34, the average age of the male respondents was 37. There was a wide mix of occupations. However, a high proportion were college educated, and 87 per cent were exclusively heterosexual. Two interesting general findings were as follows:

- Men assumed that women valued male appearance more than female respondents acknowledged (overall).
- Although most female respondents played down male appearance overall, there was a significant 'subgroup' of females for whom male physical looks was highly important. They tended to be older, professional women, who rated themselves as more physically attractive.

Figure 2.4 summarizes some of the main findings.

Commentary

Figure 2.4 highlights some interesting points regarding perceptions of male beauty.

- We must remember that the survey is American, it

therefore reflects the perceptions and values of the American culture.

- The fact that women who rate themselves as more attractive tend to place more emphasis on male looks gives support to the matching hypothesis (see p. 36). Because they see themselves as more attractive, on the whole they seek a more attractive partner.
- The fact that personality factors won 'hands down' suggests social influences overrode evolutionary imperatives. Only 20 per cent found body builders attractive and physical strength was rated lowest.
- An interesting finding was that some women commented that 'cute' men could be attractive. Some women found baldness cute. In Chapter 1 we pointed out the importance of cuteness in attachment.
- Some of the findings were not obtained from the structured questions themselves, but the unstructured comment sections. This highlights the importance of allowing 'free-response' sections when constructing questionnaires.

Male attractiveness and height

Aristotle pointed out that 'personal beauty should be tall', a sentiment still echoed today. Contemporary studies have found that height appears to be a valued characteristic in men in Western society. Not only does it increase aesthetic judgements, but it also seems to produce a 'halo effect' as well. A study conducted at the University of Pittsburgh (cited by Eysenck, 1981) showed that students who were 6' 2" or over, received an average starting salary at least 12 per cent higher than those who were under 6'. For nearly 200 years, on average, members of the US Senate have been taller than the average American male, and few US presidents have been under 6'.

However, this isn't true of all societies. History is littered with powerful male leaders who have fallen well short of the 6' mark. Deng Xiaoping of China, Attila the Hun, Napoleon Bonaparte and Adolf Hitler are just four examples. But even within the aesthetic-conscious Hollywood, shorter males still appear to 'make it big'. Mel Gibson, Mickey Rooney, Tom Cruise, Sylvester Stallone are all a lot shorter than 6'. In fact, Alan Ladd (a 'tough-guy' filmstar of the 1950s) frequently wore built-up boots to enhance his rather short stature. The American sociologist Feldman summarized the American obsession with male height by saying:

'American society is a society with a heightist premise: to be tall is to be good and to be short is to be stigmatized.'

- Personality factors came out as most important. Both male and female respondents rated intelligence and humour as most important.
- Sexual performance and physical strength were least important.
- Although the survey questionnaire did not specifically ask about personal hygiene, a substantial number of female respondents referred to it as highly important in the comment section. Dental hygiene was a particular concern.
- Male height was perceived as an asset by both males and females. However, female respondents appeared more tolerant of shorter men than the male respondents thought they would be.
- Overweight men were perceived as less attractive. However, females were again more tolerant than male respondents thought they would be. Thinner women were more concerned with male weight.
- Male muscles were perceived by male respondents as important. However, the majority of women did not find male muscles important. Only 20 per cent of female respondents acknowledged finding body builders attractive.
- Fifty-two per cent of male respondents thought women would find bald men unattractive. In fact, 40 per cent of women agreed that baldness was unattractive in men. They tended to be younger and rate themselves as more attractive. Some female respondents said they found bald men cute.
- Clean shaven faces were preferred, with 60 per cent of the male respondents being clean-shaven.
- Over 71 per cent of male and female respondents thought that males 'make too much of an issue' over penis size. Female respondents who rated themselves as highly attractive, tended to value penis size more.

Adapted from *Psychology Today*, November/December 1994

Figure 2.4: Key findings of the Psychology Today *survey regarding male attractiveness*

Commentary

As we have just seen, and as we saw in the *Psychology Today* survey above, male height is perceived as an asset by both male and females. So what is it, that makes male height so important? One explanation may be found again in evolution. Buss and Schmitt (1993) found that women rated short men as undesirable for either short-term or long-term relationships. Ellis (1992) provides further evidence for this, by showing that taller men are consistently perceived as more desirable dates than average or shorter men. Buss (1999) believes that evolution has programmed women to respond favourably to athletic prowess. Having a tall, muscular mate conveys the added benefit of protection. Whether this explanation is valid or not is in many ways irrelevant. What seems to matter is that societies appear to respond to this 'heightist agenda' (see the psychology of personal ads on p. 41).

Male height and paternity

An article appeared in *Nature* relating height to paternity. Dunbar *et al* (2000) examined the medical records of 4400 healthy men aged 25–60 who were given compulsory medical examinations in Wrocl'aw Poland, between 1983 and 1989. Their hypothesis was that because the literature suggested that taller men were more attractive to women, they would be more likely to have more children. Their results found that on average childless men were significantly shorter, taking into account age and lifestyle.

Commentary

What is interesting is that Dunbar again opts for an evolutionary explanation. He suggests height preference is 'programmed into women's genes'. He says:

'In the social sciences, people seem very reluctant to believe that evolutionary principles guide human behaviour at all. It must help to turn the tide.'

However, not all commentators agree. Barton (2000), an evolutionary biologist from the University of Durham, points out that not all cultures see height as attractive. Certain tribes such as the Guiacian of Venezuela have notoriously short warriors. This might explain why evolution has not stretched the height gap further. Barton says:

'Clearly something has limited that process.'

Beauty as a social/cultural phenomenon

Across the centuries different cultures and societies have perceived beauty in different ways. Darwin (1883) suggested that concepts of beauty were based upon cultural differences not genetics. Freud (1905) proposed that beauty was intrinsically

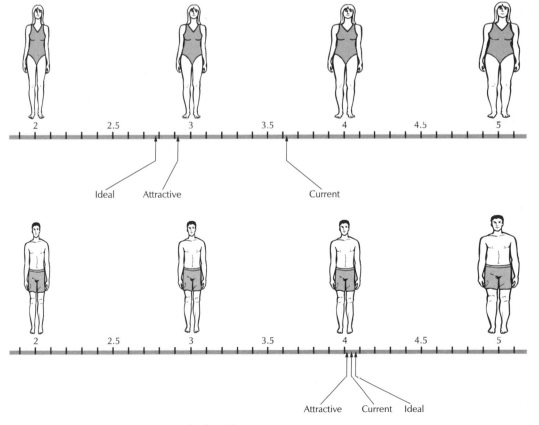

Figure 2.5: Results of Fallon and Rozin's study (1985)

linked to sexual arousal. Certain African women develop large buttocks (steatogygia) as they reach puberty, and this is seen as both attractive and desirable by males. Japanese Sumo wrestlers (who would perhaps be classed as enormous by western standards) are treated as sex symbols by many young girls within their own culture. A girlfriend of 41-stone Sumo superstar 'Konishiki' was slimmer than one of his legs. As we saw earlier in western cultures, often it is the media that define what is beautiful by engaging in 'high profile exposure' of certain looks (e.g. the 'lollipop ladies of Hollywood').

The media and perceptions of thinness

Orbach (1978) suggested that the way in which we perceive 'body shape' is intrinsically linked to wider social issues such as feminism and social identity. Indeed, many feminist writers see the perpetuation of the 'beautiful female' as exploitation by the media. Indeed, Boskind-White and White (1983) found that bulimic women tended to be overly obsessed with being attractive to men. But does Western society really place undue pressure on women to conform to certain standards of beauty? Stice and Shaw (1994) presented magazine photographs portraying ultra-thin models to female university students. They found that the women became generally more anxious and dissatisfied with their own bodies than those female participants who viewed 'average-weight' models.

Commentary

A study conducted by Fallon and Rozin (1985) asked male and female participants to identify on a linear scale, their current body shape, their ideal body shape, and the body shape they felt would be most attractive to the opposite sex. Figure 2.5 illustrates the results, and shows that on average men selected very similar figures for all three choices. Female participant selections, varied significantly.

Clearly, women appear to be more affected by perceptions of body shape than men. More recently, the British Medical Association (BMA) has voiced its concerns regarding media portrayals of thin models. Broome (1998), a former director of public health, said:

'The constant image of very thin models, encouraged girls to develop eating disorders. We urge the media to be more responsible and show more buxom wenches.'

Beauty as an evolutionary imperative

As we saw in Chapter 1, evolutionary explanations

argue that there is a relationship between certain physical characteristics and beauty. Buss (1999) suggests that perceptions of what is beautiful are not arbitrary judgements based on the fads of a culture at any given time, but are embedded in 'evolutionary practicality'. Humans need to recognize 'who will be best to mix their genes with'. Singh (1993) argued that the more curvaceous the female (lower waist–hip ratio), the more attractive she was perceived to be. This, Singh suggests, relates to levels of female fertility (see p. 10). Even features that many of us would take for granted as attractive (such as clear complexion, shiny hair, etc.) arguably have an evolutionary 'underpinning'. In an ingenious study, Gangestad and Buss (1993) tested the notion that in cultures where parasite infestation was high, more emphasis would be placed on physical attractiveness (especially in choosing a long-term mate). This hypothesis was based upon a well-known fact, that parasites 'damage' the appearance of individuals. The hypothesis was statistically confirmed. It appears that individuals who live in ecologies where parasitic infection is likely, imperfections (especially on the skin) are seen as undesirable. They are not seen as good 'breeding material'.

Commentary

Further cross-cultural evidence for this comes from the observations of the anthropologist Milinowski (1923). The Trobriand Islanders find sores or other skin eruptions repulsive from the viewpoint of erotic contact. It appears that even across cultures, lustrous hair, clear skin and bright eyes are valued commodities.

A problem with studying attraction from a cross-cultural perspective

One of the major problems with cross-cultural and anthropological studies is that their interpretations are always so heavily influenced by the cultural, social and psychological beliefs of the researchers carrying out the work. For example, whenever 'Western' anthropologists stumble across some remote tribal culture, they start making comparisons with their own social experiences. This inevitably leads to Western society being viewed as 'normal' and tribal behaviour being assessed on how far it deviates from this standard. The following extract makes this point very well.

The Hsitirb tribe

'Many in this society engage in a series of complex rituals designed to make themselves more attractive to the

opposite sex. They acquire "potions" from local suppliers, which they apply to their hair, and skin in various ways. Then ceremonial garments are tried on, often a number of times, before the right combination is obtained. It is very important within this culture that just the right look is obtained. Errors could have implications for mating prospects. Once at the special "mating ceremony", a variety of drugs are ingested, and communal and ritualistic dancing is engaged in. It is dark, hot and crowded, and the drumbeats are fast. During the ceremony it is anticipated that sexual relationships will develop.' (Apologies to Horace Miner, 1956.)

Having now read the above description, you may be wondering where this Hsitirb tribe originates from. Turn to p. 51 where an explanation is provided.

Scientific attempts at defining beauty

Some of the earliest scientific work into 'what makes an attractive face' was carried out by Langlois and Roggman (1990). They generated computer composites of the human face, then superimposed these faces upon one another to create new faces. Participants were then asked to rate the 'superimposed faces' as well as the original face. An interesting result emerged. The composite faces obtained higher ratings for attractiveness than the original single face. The researchers concluded that superimposing the same face upon itself, lots and lots of times, 'ironed out' irregularities. Therefore the more symmetrical the face, the more attractive it is perceived. Thornhill *et al* (1997) proposed that a reliable marker for good health in males is the extent to which their bodies and faces are symmetrical. Their argument is that environment and genetic stressors at any stage in development, could create deviations from this symmetry and result in unevenness.

Some researchers have even suggested there is a symmetry formula for the perfect face (see RLA 6).

Commentary

Further studies have given weight to the idea that facial symmetry could be important. Gangestad *et al* (1994) found that less symmetrical people are perceived as less attractive (this research included the whole body). Also, the older an individual, the less symmetrical they become, suggesting symmetry could be an indicator of youthfulness. A further dimension to this research was added by Shackelford and Larson (1997) when they showed that facial symmetry is positively correlated to measures of psychological and physiological health. Being symmetrical appears to be a good thing.

Real Life Application 6:
The face of beauty

Material A – the beauty formula
When Greek writings were rediscovered during the Renaissance, they illustrated many ways in which the Greeks applied mathematics to the 'art' of beauty. One highly influential idea of its time was the formula known as the 'golden section'. The Greeks believed that the most aesthetically pleasing look had a 'proportion ratio' of just over 1.6. More recently, Lowey (1994), based at University College Hospital, London, conducted detailed analysis of fashion models' proportions and found a ratio of 1.618. On beautiful hands the relationship between the shorter and longer joints is 1.618. On a beautiful face, the distance between the hairline to the tip of the nose, and the distance from the nose to the chin is both 1.618. Lowey points out that this proportion is perceived by most as very attractive, but cannot give any explanation why this figure should be so important.

Material B – consistency of beauty across cultures
Cunningham *et al* (1995) found very high levels of agreement between different races in their perceptions of facial attractiveness. In a further study, Taiwanese participants were asked to rate the original perceptions, and a very high correlation (0.91) was obtained. The authors found that the amount of exposure to Western media appeared to have no effects on the ratings.

Article adapted from *Focus* magazine, July 1994

Summary

- The Greeks originally proposed that a 'beautiful proportion' had a ratio of just over 1.6.
- Lowey (1994) analysed the proportions of fashion models and found the ratio to be 1.618.
- The origins of the ratio 1.6 are still unclear. However, it does illustrate that beauty appears to be subject to the laws of mathematics.
- Cunningham *et al* (1995) showed that people of different races and cultures, showed high consistency in perceptions of facial attractiveness, irrespective of levels of exposure to Western media.

The effects of attractive people on others

An excellent university lecturer of mine used to say that 'looks can achieve all'. In many ways this is true. The scientific literature is full of studies which appear to suggest that attractive people have a distinct advantage in the 'social arena'. One of the earliest reports of this was written by Dion et al (1972). It found that 'onlookers' tended to attribute more favourable personality characteristics to an attractive person than they did to a less attractive individual. In either case they knew nothing of the personality of the people. This phenomenon became known as the 'what is beautiful is good' stereotype. It is sometimes referred to as the 'halo effect', for obvious reasons. Outlined below are a selection of studies which demonstrate this effect further.

- Cash and Trimer (1984) found that essays were perceived to be better quality if the readers were misled into thinking the authors were more attractive.
- Dion and Dion (1987) showed that attractive people are perceived to be more interesting, more exciting, sexy and socially skilled than non-attractive individuals.
- Agnew and Thompson (1984) found participants attributed the cause of HIV infection, based upon their perceptions of the attractiveness of the sufferer. If the sufferer was viewed as attractive, then they were judged to have caught it from heterosexual contact; if they were viewed as less attractive, they were judged to have caught it from homosexual contact or sharing needles.
- It isn't just adults where the 'halo effect' seems to apply. Karraker and Stern (1990) even found that 'attractive' babies were perceived to be more sociable and competent than less attractive ones.

Commentary

There have been a number of different ideas put forward in an attempt to explain the 'halo effect'. One very simple suggestion states that good-looking people create a good mood 'within the viewer'. It is this good mood which creates the bias in attributions. Another idea suggests that attractive individuals are 'given higher social attributes' because 'average looking people' (the majority statistically speaking) are hoping that they may gain some 'social kudos' by associating with them. In this way attractive people become status symbols. Is there any evidence for this second notion?

Sigall and Landy (1973) found that average-looking men benefit from being 'paired' with attractive women. However, the assessments of women are not affected by being paired with an attractive man (Bar-Tal and Saxe, 1976). It appears that men gain the greatest kudos.

However the 'halo effect' is only part of the story. What happens when people start comparing themselves to same-sex attractive individuals?

Attractive same-sex people as comparisons

Whether we would admit it or not, all of us have a concept regarding our own level of attractiveness. Some would view themselves as highly attractive, while others would confer a low score on themselves. Perhaps most would see themselves as average. Studies have shown that people don't enjoy being compared to same-sex individuals they perceive to be more attractive than themselves. However, is this dislike justified? The answer appears to be yes.

Commentary

Kenrick et al (1993) found that when they presented a person of average attractiveness to participants who had just viewed some highly attractive people, the ratings of the 'average person' were lower than if they had been presented on their own. This suggests if you want to enhance your own looks do not go to parties full of attractive models (that is, of course, unless you are one yourself).

Self-esteem and beauty

Other studies have suggested that self-esteem can be affected by 'self comparison'. Thornton and Moore (1993) found that when participants were presented with attractive 'same-sex' models, their own self rating was decreased. Kenrick et al (1993) showed that the participants' mood could be 'deflated' while viewing attractive same-sex models, compared with average ones. However, when these same participants viewed attractive opposite-sex models, their mood became more positive.

Commentary

Studies such as Kenrick *et al*'s show that seeing attractive 'same-sex' individuals can make us feel deflated (perhaps due to feelings of inadequacy); however, viewing attractive 'opposite-sex' individuals can enhance our mood. An explanation for these results could be found in 'evolutionary theory'. Males prefer to look at attractive females because they portray 'good potential breeding partners'. Looking at attractive males presents potential competition for females, hence a decline in mood. The problem with explanations such as these is that they are totally heterosexual in focus.

Other research has shown that attractive individuals are less lonely, show lower levels of social anxiety and are more sexually experienced (Feingold, 1992). However, as we might expect, self-esteem only appears to be elevated if the individual perceives himself or herself to be attractive (Feingold, 1992). Even so, being good looking can have its drawbacks, which impinge upon self-esteem. Major *et al* (1984) found that people who believed themselves to be good looking took less credit for work they had produced, when they believed they were watched by an evaluator. It was as if they felt they were only receiving positive feedback because of their appearance. Also Krebs and Adinolfi (1975) found that the more physically attractive a person was, the more likely he or she was to be 'socially rejected' by members of his or her own sex.

Commentary

The 'common sense' view that attractive individuals will possess high self-esteem only appears to hold true if they perceive themselves to be attractive. Studies such as Major's and Kreb and Adinolfi's demonstrate that being attractive can even, potentially, adversely affect self-esteem. Even famous celebrities often find it difficult to understand why they have become 'icons of attraction'. Uma Thurman (who played the part of Poison Ivy in the film *Batman and Robin*) was quoted as saying:

'That I am found attractive is bizarre to me.'

Attraction and cognitive scoring systems

When we rate both our own level of attractiveness and others, it is highly likely we attach some sort of 'cognitive value' to our assessment. Maybe we see them as 9/10 (highly attractive), perhaps 5/10 or 6/10 (average), or 2/10 or 3/10 (not in the least physically appealing). Over the years many psychologists have argued that we may be attracted to peo-

ple who are 10/10, but if we rate ourselves as only 5/10 or 6/10 it is unlikely that we would 'end up with them' in a long-term relationship. Instead we would 'settle down' with someone nearer our own score (Berscheid and Walster, 1978). Sometimes, however, people ignore the results of comparison scoring. In the words of an amusing saying, intended for those still looking for love, 'When all else fails, drop your standards'. Indeed, research seems to back up this position (see Key Study 3).

KEY STUDY 3

Researchers: Gladue and Delaney (1990)
Aim: The aim of this study was to assess judgements of attractiveness of the opposite sex at different time intervals throughout an evening.
Method: Students were approached at a university bar, and asked to rate same-sex and opposite-sex drinkers at 9.00 pm, 10.30 pm and midnight.
Results: Opposite-sex ratings increased, the closer it got to midnight.
Conclusions: Because same-sex ratings remained very much the same, the researchers concluded that alcohol consumption was not responsible for this effect. In many ways it could be seen as a 'desperation' strategy.

Commentary

Gladue and Delaney's (1990) study suggests that if a person has not been able to attract a partner all evening, then he or she must drop his or her standards. The country and western singer Mickey Gilley sums it up nicely in the lyrics of one of his songs, 'The girls all get prettier at closing time'.

The matching hypothesis

The idea that most people end up with someone who is similar (in rating terms) to them in physical attractiveness was put to the test in a classic study by Walster *et al* (1966). They set up a 'college dance', and when students bought their tickets they were asked to complete a questionnaire about themselves. They were told their responses would be analysed by a computer to find their ideal partner (which was actually untrue). When the students bought their tickets they were covertly judged for attractiveness by independent raters, and rather than being matched using a computer program (as the students thought), they were randomly allocated a partner. The investigators were interested in how many men would ask their partners for a second date. What was found was that the best predictor of a second date was the physical looks of the women. The more attractive, the more likely it was that the men would seek a second date, regardless of the men's looks.

Commentary

Walster *et al*'s study is interesting because it does not illustrate the matching hypothesis in its simplest form. It seemed that the less attractive or average looking men were 'trying their luck' if their date for the dance was attractive. Berscheid *et al* (1971) has suggested this could have been due to the fact that the 'computer dance' was artificially created. Participants perhaps felt obliged to stay with their dates for the evening because a computer had selected them for 'compatibility'.

Other studies, on the other hand, have given more straightforward support to the matching hypothesis:

- In an attempt to redeem their 1966 results, Walster *et al* (1969) set up another 'computer dance', except this time participants were able to meet before the dance, and allowed to indicate how attractive they wished their partner to be. The results of this study did show that couples that were most attracted to one another were ones that had been rated by independent judges as similar in levels of attraction.
- Silverman (1971) asked participants to rate the levels of attractiveness of couples who were actually going out with each other, by being observed in bars or lobbies. There was a relationship between the level of attractiveness of the couple and the level of intimacy they showed to one another.
- Murstein (1972) conducted a similar study to Silverman except it did not take place in a naturalistic setting, and it did not assess the couples together. Instead photos were taken of 99 engaged couples (or couples in long-term relationships) and compared with a similar number of random individuals. It was found that naïve judges were able to significantly assess 'who belonged to whom'. It seems that couples choose partners of a similar standard of physical appearance to themselves.

So the evidence for the matching hypothesis appears to be quite strong. However, as Walster's (1966) study shows the concept of rating self and others can be affected by other factors. Similarity does not just have to be in terms of appearance. There is considerable evidence that people who share similar attitudes and beliefs are attracted to one another.

Similarity

'Birds of a feather flock together'?

It may sound an obvious statement, but we tend to be attracted to those people who are similar to ourselves. Byrne (1961) conducted an interesting study in which students were asked to complete a questionnaire, assessing their attitudes to a number of issues. Two weeks later the researchers presented them with a completed questionnaire of a person they believed to be genuine, but who was in fact fictitious. They were asked to rate for a number of characteristics including level of attractiveness, and how much they would like to meet the individual. Byrne had cleverly manipulated the results of the fictitious person to provide four conditions:

1 The participants were presented with exactly the same attitudes they had shown two weeks earlier.
2 The participants were presented with completely opposite attitudes they had shown two weeks earlier.
3 The participants were presented with attitudes which matched their own on important issues such as religion and politics, but were the opposite in areas they themselves had rated as less important.
4 The participants were presented with attitudes which differed from their own on important issues, but matched them on less important issues (again the importance of the issues had been indicated by the participants).

The results showed that the fictitious individuals were rated as more attractive and liked more, the closer their attitudes were to the participants. Also, it appeared that they were more attracted to individuals who shared similar attitudes on important issues, rather than trivial ones.

Commentary

However, some evidence suggests that similarity of attitudes is not as important as knowing that a person likes you. Aronson (1980) showed that levels of attraction were affected more by knowing that the other person liked them, than by knowing that they held similar attitudes. In fact, even if the other person held completely opposite attitudes but showed attraction towards the other, that was enough to generate a reciprocal response.

Rubin (1973) found that American married couples were significantly similar in their attitudes to both sociological factors (such as politics, religion, etc.) and even physical factors (such as eye colour). However, the problem with findings such as these is that they do not identify at what stage the similarities took place. Were the couples initially similar (and that's what attracted them to each other in the first place), or did they 'grow' more similar having spent more time together?

Commentary

Hill *et al* (1976) found high levels of similarity for dating couples on a range of factors, almost identical to those identified by Rubin. Their study also found that the initial level of similarity between couples was a good predictor of whether they would still be together one year later. The evidence that 'birds of a feather flock together' is therefore good.

Complementarity

'Opposites attract'

The old saying 'Opposites attract' is not quite what psychologists have found. Perhaps the saying ought to be 'Those who fill in the gaps where we're deficient attract'. In Chapter 1, when we considered equity theory, we saw that an equitable relationship is one where each person gets out 'qualities' that are important to them. Often 'a quality' could be something that the individual feels personally deficient in. For example, I might be attracted to someone who is a talented cook, or an accomplished pianist (due to the fact I'm not very good at either of these things). Winch (1958) put forward the complementary needs hypothesis. The research was based upon long-term relationships such as married couples, and found many instances where complementary characteristics were evident.

Commentary

Strong *et al* (1988) attempted to identify what pairs of personality traits bring about complimentarity. Unfortunately, they did not meet with much success. There appears to be much more evidence for similarity than there does complimentarity. The evidence for 'opposites attract' is weak.

Familiarity

'Familiarity breeds contempt'

Zajonc (1968) put forward the idea that being familiar with someone increases attraction – this he termed the 'mere exposure effect'. He presented photographs of unknown faces to participants and asked them to rate them in terms of how much they felt they would like the individual. The lowest attractiveness ratings were given by participants who had never seen the photographs before, the highest by participants who had seen the photos most often. It seems that people get to like someone the more times they are exposed to them (see Figure 2.6).

Commentary

Newcomb (1961) conducted a 'real life', field experiment, in which male students were offered free board for a year in a large house at the University of Michigan, in exchange for their participation in the study. On the basis of the results of detailed questionnaires, the students were assigned roommates who were similar to themselves. The results of this study were as predicted, those who held similar attitudes became better friends than those who did not. However when the study was repeated a year later with a new group of male students, an intriguing new finding emerged. Rather than similarity being the key factor, simple familiarity appeared to determine the level of liking. The students became friends with their roommates, even when there was an inconsistency in attitudes. The evidence for 'familiarity breeds contempt' appears to be non-existent. Familiarity appears to 'breed attraction'.

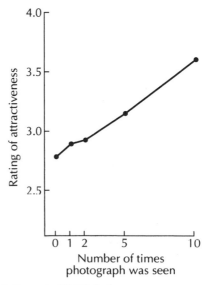

Figure 2.6: Zajonc's (1968) findings

Fallibility

'Everyone loves a fool'

As we pointed out at the beginning of this section, we can be attracted to someone for numerous reasons. One of the more interesting reasons is 'perceived fallibility'. Watching people make fools of themselves at a social gathering (perhaps by spilling their drink or tripping over) can engender either feelings of sympathy or disdain from the observer. Helmreich *et al* (1970) found that there was an interesting relationship between self-esteem, competence and attraction. Both high scorers and low scorers on personal self-esteem rated someone they perceived to be superior in status as less attractive if they made mistakes. This effect did not seem to be present in those who rated themselves as average on personal self-esteem. It was as if those with low self-esteem felt somehow cheated that this person they looked up to was incompetent, and that those with high self-esteem felt annoyed that the person wasn't living up to their high expectations. Considering that most of the population have an average level of self-esteem, it should not be too surprising when we hear of famous people's popularity ratings going up when they show themselves as fallible – so it is true that 'everyone loves a fool'?, on the whole yes.

Commentary

So what have we learnt about similarity, complementarity, familiarity and fallibility? In terms of their apparent contribution towards attraction the rankings appear to be as follows:

1st Familiarity increases attraction.
2nd We are attracted to people who hold similar attitudes to us.
3rd Someone with average self-esteem finds an individual who shows themselves to be fallible as more attractive.
4th Having complementarity characteristics on the whole does not increase attraction.

Non-verbal communication (NVC)

There are certain cues which help inform perceptions of attractiveness. These are referred to as non-verbal cues, part of a wider topic known as NVC. Argyle (1988) argues that:

'non-verbal cues for interpersonal attraction are far more powerful than initially similar verbal ones'.

He equates this to our pre-verbal ancestry, for which

KEY STUDY 4

Researchers:	Givens (1983) and Perper (1985)
Aim:	The aim of both studies was to identify stages of non-verbal behaviour within 'chat-up' scenarios.
Method:	Both studies were based upon careful observations of couples, in bars in America.
Results:	The investigators proposed that American singles bar courtship had five stages. These were:

  i   attention getting – males and females differed in their tactics here

  ii recognition – this is where the potential lovers recognized the sexual signals

  iii talk stage – this was where ice-breaking 'small talk' determined the future of the liaison

  iv touching – this is a highly intimate behaviour and only seen if the relationship was progressing well

  v   body synchrony – this was observed when couples were really comfortable. It consisted of both partners moving together, frequently mirroring each others' movements and gestures.

Conclusions:	Both studies concluded two points. Because of the common themes observed, the stages in human courtship are universal. Secondly, there are parallels to courtship behaviour found in other animal species.

---

signalling was the only means of communication. Unfortunately, this topic is so vast that we have neither the time nor space to consider it all here. Instead we have selected a few of the lesser-known studies, and related them to attraction. We will start by looking at NVC within 'chat-up' scenarios, then at facial

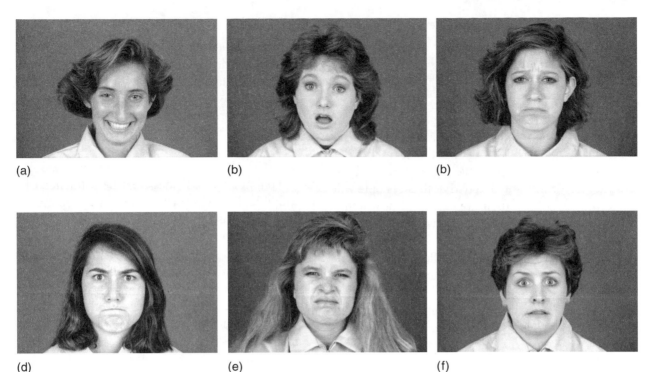

(a)   (b)   (b)

(d)   (e)   (f)

Figure 2.7: The photographs of facial expressions used in Ekman et al's (1987) study

expression, then go on to look at dress code, style of walking, glasses and the effect of first names.

NVC within 'chat-up' scenarios

David Givens, an anthropologist, and Timothy Perper, a biologist, have spent hundreds of hours observing non-verbal cues in singles bars throughout America. Their research has suggested that 'chat-up' behaviour progresses through a series of stages (see Key Study 4).

Facial expressions

One way in which we judge whether to approach individuals or not is to look at their facial expression. Darwin (1872) proposed that the perception of facial expression is innate, therefore universal. Further evidence seems to suggest this is the case. Ekman *et al* (1987) showed photographs of different facial expressions to participants from ten different countries. There was a significantly high level of agreement as to what the expressions represented (see Figure 2.7).

Commentary

Imagine you were at a party. Which of Ekman's facial expressions shown in Figure 2.7 would you feel com-

fortable to approach? Darwin (1872) believed that emotions that are perceived to be anger (therefore potentially dangerous) are recognized more effectively than happy or neutral expressions. Interestingly, there is experimental evidence that this is true. Hansen and Hansen (1988) found that participants were able to identify angry faces in photographs of crowds more quicky than happy or neutral faces.

Dress code

The scientific literature is full of studies that have investigated the effects of clothes on observers' perceptions. Gibbins (1969) asked 15- and 16-year-old girls to give their judgements regarding six photographs of people, dressed in different outfits. The amount of agreement on certain features was significantly high. These features included whether the person was:

- shy
- a smoker
- a drinker
- sporty or artistic.

Kaiser (1985) argued that clothes are most frequently evaluated in terms of the following:

- How attractive they make the person look.
- How expensive the clothes look.
- How neat the outfit makes the person appear.
- How fashionable the outfit makes the person appear.

Despite the great majority of people adopting conventional fashion trends, there are always some who deliberately like to 'kick ' against the norm. Snyder and Fromkin (1980) identified this as a need for uniqueness. It is highly likely that these people will stand out in terms of their appearance, but whether they would be perceived as attractive would depend upon the attitudes of the observer.

Sometimes appearance can affect the way in which observers perceive competence. Smart dress is frequently associated with intelligence and ability (Molloy, 1977). This effect was neatly demonstrated in a study looking at perceptions of doctors' ability.

'Smart' doctors

McKinstry and Wang (1991) showed pictures of interactions between doctors and patients. In one condition the doctor wore smart formal clothes, in the other casual informal attire. Participants were asked to rate how happy they would be to see the doctor, and how much confidence they would have in his or her ability. The results showed a significant bias towards formal dress.

Commentary

In McKinstry and Wang's study the following results were obtained:

- 44 per cent thought the male doctor should wear a suit, and 67 per cent thought he should wear a tie.
- 59 per cent would object to a male doctor wearing jeans, 55 per cent to him wearing an earring, and 46 per cent to him having long hair.
- 57 per cent felt female doctors should usually wear a skirt, 63 per cent objected to female doctors wearing jeans and 60 per cent objected to them wearing lots of jewellery.

Research such as this illustrates an interesting interaction between liking and perceived ability. In professional settings 'smart dress' equates with perceived competence.

Walking style

Montepare et al (1988) found that people were judged as more attractive if their gait (walking style) was youthful rather than elderly, regardless of the sex or age of the individual.

Glasses

Husart and Hutchinson (1993) found that both males and females are perceived to be more attractive without glasses. However, Edwards (1987) found that individuals who wear glasses are perceived to be more intelligent.

Names

Garwood et al (1980) demonstrated that people's judgements of attractiveness can be influenced by an individual's name. They asked participants to rate photographs of women for levels of attractiveness. In one condition they gave a desirable first name (such as Kathy or Jennifer) and in the other condition an undesirable name (such as Gertrude or Ethel). They found that even though it was the same person on the photograph, when an undesirable name was attached they were rated as less attractive. Colman et al (1981) found that there was a significant positive correlation between familiarity with, and liking for, male forenames. The more familiar the first name, the more it was liked.

Commentary

Evidence such as the studies cited above suggests that a non-myopic person with a 'youthful walk', and a desirable and familiar name would have a significant advantage in the attraction stakes. However, these factors are usually researched 'out of context'. As we have seen so far, other issues contribute to the attraction equation. For example, an individual may have had good past experiences with someone who wears glasses, therefore to that person wearing glasses has positive associations.

Self disclosure

Self disclosure is the term given to the process by which individuals share information with others. When we meet someone at a social gathering, we may find ourselves attracted to a person for all the reasons mentioned earlier. However, it is only when we start to converse with the individual that we really know whether we want to pursue this relationship or not. Cunningham et al (1986) suggested that 'reciprocal self disclosure' was the most effective strategy for attraction to take place. That is, we adapt our own rate of self disclosure to mirror the other person. Different cultures and societies have implicit rules as to how self disclosure unravels. Knapp (1984) found that initially couples engage in neutral topics (more commonly referred to as 'small talk'). This allows time for other assessments to be made about the potential suitability of the other person. Deep, personal self disclosure at this fragile stage of the relationship can be off-putting to the receiver.

Commentary

Research into self disclosure has highlighted a number of points.

- The context in which self disclosure takes place. It is likely people will disclose more personal information to professionals such as doctors or lawyers, and at a much quicker rate, than they would social acquaintances.
- Women tend to self disclose more information than men.
- The more we perceive a person to be trustworthy, the more we are prepared to self disclose.

The psychology of 'personal ads'

One of the best places to analyse the psychology of attraction is in the 'personal ads', or more precisely the 'lonely hearts columns'. Kenrick and Keefe (1992) examined more than 1000 lonely heart ads from America, Holland and India. They concluded the following points

- Older males seek younger women.
- Females tend to seek men who are on average about five years older than themselves.

Waynforth and Dunbar analysed approximately 900 ads in four American newspapers and found the following:

- Males were more likely to seek youthful females (42 per cent, as opposed to 25 per cent for women seeking youthful men).
- Males were more likely to seek attractive females (44 per cent, as opposed to 22 per cent for women seeking attractive men).
- Women tended to use more positive descriptions of themselves (e.g. curvaceous, pretty or gorgeous) than comparative descriptions for men (handsome, hunky, etc.), 50 per cent compared to 34 per cent.
- Women tended to specify their requirements for potential partners more than men; however, males would be more likely to disclose their postal address if it was more upmarket.

Lynn and Shurgot (1984) showed that taller men got more responses to personal ads than shorter men. Shorter men tend not to state their height in ads.

All these findings are very interesting, but once again very heterosexual. Do these 'selling points and requests' change when homosexual relationships are considered? To answer this question, Waynforth and Dunbar again examined personal ads, but this time in American 'gay newspapers', and compared

Real Life Application 7: Finding a partner in the personal ads

Figure 2.8 shows a selection of genuine personal ads, taken from a local newspaper.

SINGLE mum 37, GSOH, enjoys nights in/out and dancing, seeks male 25–40, for fun times and friendship.
TALL, slim female, mid 30s, very romantic, seeks male for love, romance, LTR, romance and more romance, must love children.
CHRISTIAN lady 52, WLTM similar N/S Christian male GSOH, kind, caring and affectionate for friendship possible relationship.
ROMANTIC Piscean lady 46, 5'2, size 10, blonde, seeks romantic male, who enjoys reading, writing poetry, dining in, cooking, walking, theatre, opera.
BLONDE, attractive, slim, funny, what more could you want? Female seeks special male 36–43, slim, tallish.
MISS Piggy, seeks Kermit, female 22 WLTM male 22–35 for fun, laughs and much more.
ATTRACTIVE female 19, let down in past, seeks older male 22–28, must be caring, loving and genuine.
SINGLE mum 25, seeks genuine male 25–35, for socialising, nights in/out, motor-cycles, friendship possible relationship.

GENTLEMAN 38, 6', blue eyes, genuine GSOH, enjoys walking dog, riding motor bike, seeks genuine female, to share evenings and weekends in/out.
SLIM, sexy, professional guy, 31, seeks attractive, slimish, normal female for good times, hurry before its too late.
PROFESSIONAL male 45, 5'6, seeks caring, honest female 25–45, GSOH essential, for LTR.
DIFFERENT! That got your attention. Male 23, 6'2, curly hair, brown eyes, enjoys nights in/out, seeks similar female 20–25 for friendship possible relationship.
SHY male 19, 5'11, blonde hair, brown eyes, seeks friends to hang around with.
TALL, slim male 30s, OHOC, very romantic, seeks slim female for love, romance, LTR possibly more, single mums welcome.
LADIES are you 20–50, slim, intelligent, happy? Professional male 41, 5'11, slim, fit, cheerful, WLTM you.
PROFESSIONAL male 25, attractive, generous, caring, honest, independent, GSOH, seeks attractive, independent female with GSOH.

Figure 2.8: Personal ads taken from The Citizen, *Thursday 27 April 2000.*

them to mainstream ones. The following points were noted:

- Heterosexual women were three times more likely to seek resources than lesbians, in their ideal partner.
- Heterosexual women were four times more likely to provide clues to their attractiveness, than lesbians.
- Homosexual men advertised resources only about half as often as heterosexual men.

Commentary

Dunbar (1995) explains these findings in terms of evolution. He argues that:

'... each individual is (unconsciously) trying to maximize his or her own contribution to the species gene pool, by producing as many great-great-grandchildren as possible'.

He goes on to point out that men and women want different things out of reproduction, hence the differences in the wording of the ads. Women want security and resources, men want the most attractive mate. He uses this difference between male and female to substantiate the differences in gay ads. They are not seeking partners for reproduction. He states:

'Lift the constraint on reproduction, and priorities change.'

Summary

- Personal ads illustrate that there are sex differences in the type of information male and female advertisers disclose.

Questions

1 Identify what percentage of males are seeking younger females.

2 Identify what percentage of females use more positive descriptions of themselves. Compare this to the percentage of males doing the same thing. What sort of words do people use to describe themselves?

3 What percentage of males give clues to their status? Compare this to the percentage of females doing the same thing.

4 How many males state their height?

Maintaining relationships

Building a future

Once the initial stages of attraction have passed, the next phase of the process is to keep the relationship going. Some of the most rewarding relationships are with people we have known for many years. However, researchers such as Duck (1992) claim that relationships are much more about the 'beliefs' couples have of the future. Making plans together, building a future based upon 'psychological investment' seems to be a good indicator of long-term success. It seems logical that predictions about the future of relationships would be based upon years of shared memories. However, Miell (1987) has shown that individuals are often more influenced by the past three days of their relationship than years of experiences. More evidence that 'beliefs' are a crucial factor in the maintenance of relationships comes from Duck and Sants (1983). They suggest that:

'relationships have their permanence in the mind'.

In other words, if people keep thinking about another person, distance and frequency of face-to-face exchanges ceases to be an issue. In Chapter 4 we consider how religious hermits are able to live a life of isolation (see p. 76). Their belief in a close relationship with God allows them to devote themselves completely to religious service.

Commentary

As we have seen, the beliefs couples have regarding their relationship can determine its ultimate success. Emotional investment, and planning for the future can provide a relationship with direction and purpose. Often, when common goals are achieved or taken away (as in the case of winning large sums of money), couples find themselves devoid of purpose. The 'striving together' to achieve something has been removed.

Strategies for maintaining relationships

Ayres (1983) administered questionnaires to a large sample of couples in an attempt to identify the strategies they used to keep their relationships going. Three distinct categories emerged. Below is an outline of each category, and a fictitious example, to help illustrate the points.

1 **Avoidance** – this is where one of the couple wishes to develop the relationship, but the other

does not. The other person is happy for it to remain at its present level, and frequently 'avoids' attempts to take things further.

Lucy and John have been going out with each other for six months. John is very keen to move in with Lucy, but Lucy values her independence. Every time John tries to talk about the future of their relationship, Lucy tells him to stop being so serious and just enjoy himself. Her favourite saying, which she keeps quoting to John, is 'Just relax, and take each day as it comes'. However, John is getting more and more anxious.

2 **Balance** – this is where one of the couple is happy to let the relationship 'deteriorate'. The other person tries desperately hard to 'balance' the situation by over-compensating for his or her partner's lack of effort.

Philip and Angela have being going out with each other for the past three months. Right from the start it was evident that Angela was not as keen as Philip. However, the relationship continued. Recently, Angela has appeared to lose interest altogether. Philip, on the other hand, has tried every strategy he can to keep the relationship going. He has paid for an expensive weekend away, he has had flowers delivered to her office, and most recently he has bought her a brand new car. At the moment Angela remains with Philip.

3 **Directness** – this is where one of the couple is open and honest about the future of the relationship to the other.

Paul and Steve have been living together for the past 12 months. Paul is homosexual and has been attracted to Steve ever since he moved in as a flatmate. Steve is aware of the situation, but being heterosexual has no interest in Paul, other than as a friend. He has spent many hours explaining the situation, being honest with Paul. Paul appears to have got the message, as recently he introduced Steve to his new boyfriend.

Commentary

Other studies have found that different factors influence which strategy is used. For example, Shea and Pearson (1986) found that women preferred to use a 'direct approach' when explaining to their male partners that they were not interested in taking the relationship further.

Routine as a maintenance strategy

It may sound inconceivable, but routine can help in the process of maintaining relationships. It must be made clear, however, that we are referring to 'routine' as in the sense of habit, not as some may interpret it, as 'being bored'. Boredom is a different matter altogether and will be considered in the next section, under relationship breakdown. Most of us in our everyday lives take the trivia that occurs within our relationships for granted. Morgan (1986) suggested that it is only when relationships break down, that people start to notice these minor points. In many ways it is a classic case of 'you don't know what you've got until it's gone syndrome'. It is these virtually unnoticed activities that help to 'glue' couples together.

Commentary

Dindia and Baxter (1987) found that the longer couples had been married, the fewer maintenance strategies they engaged in (such as paying each other compliments or reminiscing together). It was as if the relationship was able to be maintained through simple routine. Duck (1990) summarizes this point well when he says:

'The remarkable fact about daily life is that continuities exist and do not have to be worked for, once the relationship is defined and established.'

Social and cultural influences in the maintenance of relationships

The role of society and expectations of different cultures must not be forgotten when considering the maintenance of relationships. Ginsburg (1988) argues that different cultures have rules and scripts that influence the course and development of relationships. Duck (1992) points out that in Western society we develop implicit clues as to how to conduct relationships. We know for instance what is perceived as good publicity and what is seen as bad.

'We try to hide affairs and hope that newspapers do not find out about them, but we are happy to publicise marriages in those self-same newspapers.' (Duck, 1992)

Hagestad and Smyer (1982) considered the role 'social context' has to play in the maintenance (or ultimate breakdown) of relationships. Often people stay in a relationship because they feel that is what society expects. When couples have children, and develop social networks with similar friends, they become part of the 'family scene'. The fact they are a family as well as a couple becomes reinforced by social norms, making things very complicated if break-up occurs.

Commentary

In some cultures more than others, the issue of maintaining relationships is helped by social norms. Zulu men, for example, are allowed to marry more than one wife (polygamy). Elliott (1978), who studied the Zulu culture for many years, concluded that the wives do get jealous of each other from time to time; however, Zulu men have a unique way of dealing with it. Elliott quotes the words of a Zulu chief:

'Sometimes they don't fight much, and if they do, their husband gives them a good beating, and that stops them.'

Clearly, there are many ways of maintaining relationships. The question, however, should perhaps be more about quality, rather than duration.

Factors which make relationships successful

As we have seen above, maintaining relationships should be all about quality. One way of achieving this is to analyse the factors which make relationships successful. Duck (1992) reviewed a number of studies which looked at marital satisfaction and identified the following issues. Happily married couples were:

- more willing to talk about their relationship together
- gave each other more positive and consistent non-verbal cues (compared with unhappy couples)
- were more likely to compromise when problems arose.

Lauer and Lauer (1985) questioned hundreds of couples (who had been married for a minimum of 15 years) to identify reasons as to why they felt their marriages had lasted. Four key features consistently emerged. They were:

1 friendship – the couples felt that their partners were also their best friends
2 similarity – the couples regarded themselves as well suited
3 commitment – the couples were prepared to make the relationship work, and ironically this was reinforced by the fact they were still together
4 positive reinforcement – many couples commented on how being with each other made them

feel happy. They shared their emotional states with each other, and it was this that made them feel close.

Different styles of marriage

Johnson *et al* (1992) studied married couples (those who had been married for approximately two years), and questioned them regarding the ways in which they organized their daily lives. The researchers identified four distinct patterns. Table 2.1 outlines the key features.

Commentary

Two interesting findings which emerged from Johnson *et al*'s work were as follows:

- There was a consistent level of marital satisfaction across the four groups. This could be due to the dynamics of the relationships formed, through the mutual consent of each partner. In other words, both partners were happy with the sort of relationship they had created.
- When it came to parenthood, significant differences emerged. After two years, 35.7 per cent of the symmetrical type marriages were likely to have children

Table 2.1: Characteristics of different marriage styles, based upon Johnson et al *(1992)*

Type of marriage	Characteristics of marriage
Symmetrical 42%	<ul><li>Husband and wife both have jobs.</li><li>Household tasks are not sex-typed.</li><li>Sex role ideology is egalitarian.</li><li>Spouses spend little leisure time together.</li><li>35.7% have children.</li></ul>
Parallel 27%	<ul><li>Husband is primary wage earner.</li><li>Housework is divided in sex-typed way.</li><li>Spouses spend little time together.</li><li>Husband spends time with friends.</li><li>Wife spends time with relatives.</li><li>77.8% have children.</li></ul>
Differentiated 21%	<ul><li>Both work; husband's job emphasized.</li><li>Housework is divided in sex-typed way.</li><li>Spouses spend most leisure time together and are equally involved with friends and relatives.</li><li>71.4% have children.</li></ul>
Reversed 10%	<ul><li>Wife is involved with outside job.</li><li>Household jobs are not sex-typed.</li><li>Relationship is highly companionate.</li><li>Husband spends time with friends and relatives.</li><li>50% have children.</li></ul>

followed by approximately 50 per cent of the reversed type marriages, then 71.4 per cent of the differentiated and 77.8 per cent of the parallel type. Clearly, the domestic arrangements of the couples dictated the likelihood of children.

So far we have considered the initial process of attraction and what keeps the relationship going. Finally, we need to turn our attention to why things go wrong.

The breakdown of relationships

Reasons why relationships go wrong

It is obvious that relationships go wrong for many reasons. One way of analysing these is to consider the opposite perspective of attraction. Figure 2.9 (below) takes some of the key theories of attraction and does just this.

Duck (1981) suggests the reasons for relationship breakdown fall into two groups:

1 Predisposing personal factors – these would include irritating personal habits or personality characteristics. Again, in the early stages of the relationship these may not have been apparent.
2 Precipitating factors – these would include external influences such as heavy work commitments, financial difficulties and interference from third parties.

Physical looks

Attraction towards a partner can change over time. Obviously, looks deteriorate over time. Also, as the *Psychology Today* survey found (see p. 30), both males and females valued personality characteristics such as intelligence and humour as being most important. Obviously, it takes time to assess these factors. Getting the initial looks right but the personality wrong can in the long term lead to breakdown.

The matching hypothesis

As we saw earlier in this chapter, some researchers suggest that we end up with those people who roughly match us in physical looks. Sometimes, however, there are exceptions to this rule. One partner may be highly attractive, while the other is not so fortunate. If, as equity theory states, this mismatch is compensated for in other ways, then the relationship should be all right. However, this is where equity theory has to be taken a stage further. Over time people's views change. Indeed, their physical looks change. What may have started out as a balanced situation, in time could become imbalanced.

Similarity

The same argument we have just used applies to similarity. Over time attitudes change. This is all right as long as both partners change in the same direction and at the same speed. Because people tend to change more in their younger years, this could explain why marrying too young increases the risk of separation and divorce (Fisher, 1992).

Complementarity

As we saw when we considered this in relation to attraction, the evidence appears to be weak. It is more likely therefore that holding opposing views is actually a factor that facilitates breakdown not attraction. Couples often state after splitting up that they had nothing in common. The intriguing question is 'did they ever', or did they just 'grow apart'?

Familiarity

Losing touch with someone can lead to relationship breakdown. Cardwell *et al* (2000) cites geographical separation as a reason why relationships come to an end. Young people going away to university have to work very hard to keep existing romantic relationships going. For the same reason that being familiar with someone increases attraction, being distanced from them can lead to problems. In the case of students there is the added problem of all the potential new people they will meet!

Fallibility

What may have been an endearing quality (such as clumsiness, etc.) in the initial stages of the relationship could, in time, become a major source of irritation.

Figure 2.9: When attraction 'goes wrong'

Assessing levels of personal investment

Sometimes, it was inevitable from the start that a particular couple were not 'going to last'. Perhaps one of the couple was 'giving' more than the other. We saw in Chapter 1 that equity theory (Homans, 1974) states that in order for a relationship to last, both partners need to feel they are getting out roughly what they are putting in (see p. 25). If this situation changes breakdown is likely to ensue. Rusbult (1983) found that an accurate predictor of relationship stability was the amount of investment an individual perceived he or she had given to a relationship. The more a person felt he or she had invested, the more likely he or she would stick with it. More recently, Rusbult and Martz (1995) found that women were more likely to remain in abusive relationships if they perceived alternatives to be poor and their own investment to be high.

Commentary

Rusbult (1987) took this idea of investment further by identifying the potential strategies open to people when they realize there is an 'investment imbalance'. She identified four responses:

1 **Voice** – this is where the individual 'voices' his or her concerns regarding the imbalance.
2 **Loyalty** – this is where the individual tolerates the imbalance, and learns to accept it. Both these approaches are active strategies. However, she goes on to identify two passive ones.
3 **Neglect** – because of the imbalance, the individual loses interest in the relationship.
4 **Exit** – no attempt is made to reconcile the imbalance, the individual just leaves.

Psychologists can use these active and passive strategies to analyse how different groups of people deal with

Initial breakdown – dissatisfaction with relationship

In this first stage a partner (or partners) become distressed at the way in which the relationship is going. Duck suggests a threshold is reached in which a person feels action must be taken – 'I can't stand this anymore'.

Intra-psychic phase – a 'brooding focus'

In this second stage the individual deals with the difficulties in private or by sharing them with a trusted friend. Evaluations regarding the relationship and plans for the future are made within the individual's mind. This time a threshold is reached in which a person feels 'I would be justified in withdrawing'.

Dyadic phase – the confrontation

Duck proposes that sooner or later couples must confront one another to discuss the future of their relationship. This third stage can lead either to reconciliation or break-up.

There is evidence from other researchers that often this phase is actually missed out. Lee (1984) and Baxter (1984) found that people often leave relationships without explicitly telling the other person. 'I'll phone you' or 'Let's stay friends' are frequently used expressions, in order to avoid direct dissolution.

Social phase – telling others about the decision

In this fourth stage a couple's decision to 'split up' is made public. Duck suggests we need others on our side during the ensuing reorganization. Often friends of the couple have to decide where their loyalties lie. Friends can also provide 'cognitive reinforcement' during this stage. Phrases such as 'I always thought you were too good for him' and 'She was a nasty person' are good examples. Duck suggests that at this stage a 'point of no return' is reached – 'It's now inevitable'.

Grave-dressing phase – 'burying the past'

The final stage is all about forgetting the past. Individuals start to create stories that emphasize that the relationship is finished.

There is further evidence that suggests that the social and grave-dressing phases are the last stages of relationship breakdown. La Gaipa (1982) found that 'gossip' with social networks reinforces opinions regarding partners. Each time a person leaves a relationship he or she needs to leave with what La Gaipa refers to as 'social credit', that is a good reputation. It is sometimes easier for both parties to admit simply that they were not suited than to suggest that either one of them had a social problem.

Figure 2.10: The stages of breakdown, based upon Duck (1984)

potential breakdown. Certainly Rusbult *et al* (1990) found a correlation between self-esteem and dissolution strategy. Those people with high self-esteem responded to relationship failure by exiting, those with low self-esteem engaged in passive neglect. It may be that some cultures tend to use a passive approach, while others prefer an active stance. Maybe there are age or sex differences in preferred strategy. These are questions for further research.

The dynamic nature of relationship breakdown

Most psychologists would agree that relationship breakdown is a process not an event. Duck (1984) developed a framework to analyse this process. Figure 2.10 identifies the stages and gives a brief explanation.

Commentary

Both Lee (1984) and Baxter (1984) presented stage theories of their own regarding the dissolution of relationships. Below both theories are outlined.

Lee (1984)

The five stages involved in breaking off a long-term romantic relationship are as follows:
1 The dissatisfaction is discovered. (D)
2 The dissatisfaction is exposed. (E)
3 There is negotiation between the couple. (N)
4 There is an attempt to resolve the problems. (R)
5 The relationship is transformed. (T)

Baxter (1984)

Baxter looked specifically at how couples disengage from a dysfunctional relationship. He proposed six distinct stages as follows:
1 Onset of difficulties.
2 An individual decides to leave.
3 The individual engages in disengagement behaviour.
4 The other person in the couple reacts to the other's behaviour.
5 Attempts may be made to reconcile, however are not successful.
6 Both engage in disengagement behaviour – both accept it's all over.

If you compare Lee's and Baxter's theories with Duck's you will see that there are both similarities and differences. One difference (that has already been highlighted in Figure 2.10) is that Lee (1984) found that often people move directly from stage N to T. That is, they make no attempt to reconcile. If you recall, Duck suggests that all 'breakdown scenarios' have a dyadic phase – that is couples engage in dialogue to save their relationships.

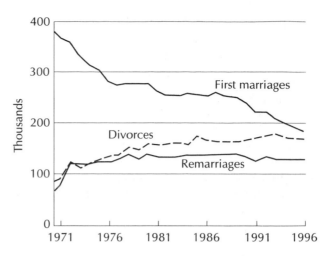

Figure 2.11: UK marriages and divorces between 1970 and 1996 (Source: 'Marriages and divorces,' Office for National Statistics © Crown Copyright 2000)

Divorce

It is a sad fact but in 1992 approximately 50 per cent of first marriages in America ended in divorce. However, Duck (1992) makes the interesting point that conversely this means that 50 per cent endured. In Britain the number of divorces taking place between 1970 and 1996 more than doubled to 171,000. As can be seen from Figure 2.11, the divorce rate peaked in 1993.

Social explanations of divorce

But what could account for this increase? Some commentators suggest that there has been a steady breakdown of 'family values'. In fact, the Chancellor of the Exchequer Gordon Brown introduced tax benefits in favour of those with 'traditional' family units in 1999, clearly showing the government's 'pro-family value' philosophy.

Twenty-four hour culture

It may be argued, however, that the increase in divorce is due to 'structural' changes within society. Modern Western society has become a 24-hour culture, that expects everything to be quick and efficient. Martin Moore-Ede (1993) sums up the concern many scientists have when he says:

'The most obvious are the costs of stresses on family life when one or both parents work around the clock.'

He goes on to point out the devastating effect this can have on relationships between partners and parents and children. Tepas (1992) found that the divorce rate in shift workers was 60 per cent higher compared to day workers in regular jobs. The 24-hour culture also applies to the speed at which divorce takes place. As Wilson (1993) puts it:

'Marriage, once a sacrament, has become in the eyes of the law a contract that is easily negotiated, re-negotiated or rescinded.'

He goes on to talk about the philosophy of a 'no-fault' divorce, which would have been unthinkable up until a few years ago (Glendon, 1991). In fact, the Matrimonial and Family Proceedings Act 1984 made it easier to obtain a divorce, by reducing the period of petitioning from three years to one.

Commentary

The theories considered so far stress the social and structural components which contribute to increased divorce rates. Further social evidence comes from cross-cultural studies into divorce. Figure 2.12 illustrates some of these differences.

Social reasons for divorce

Clearly, it would be wrong to suggest that there is a finite list of reasons why people get divorced. Every

- The eleventh-century Islamic scholar al-Ghazali pronounced that divorce was easy to obtain. A man had to say aloud 'I divorce thee' three times. Today these divorce procedures still exist in much of the Islamic Arab world. They are referred to as 'talaq'. Islamic law also gives rulings as to when it is appropriate for a woman to leave her husband.
- Anthropologists have studied divorce in the Kung Bushmen of the Kalahari Desert. Women provide much of the food, and have rights to water supplies. This gives them much status in Kung society. When marriages go wrong, either the male or the female packs his or her belongings and moves on to another camp. Howell (1979) found that out of 331 Kung marriages studied, 134 ended in divorce. Some Kung women had as many as five different spouses.
- In some cultures divorce rates are low. Japan has a low divorce rate, compared with the USA and Britain (Cornell, 1989). Many agricultural societies such as India and China have low divorce rates (Dupâquier, 1984).

Figure 2.12: Cross-cultural example of divorce

couple is different, and so too are every set of circumstances. However, scientists have identified certain factors which pre-dispose couples to divorce. The interesting thing is these appear universal (Fisher, 1992).

- Betzig (1989) found that in an analysis of 160 societies, philandering (particularly by the female), was the main cause of marital break-up. Sterility and barrenness was identified in second place, with violence appearing third. A whole range of specific personality traits were identified next (including behaviours such as laziness, jealousy, etc.).
- Fisher (1992) conducted research into the divorce rates of 62 countries from 1947 to 1989. She found that contrary to the popular myth, there is a 'four-year itch' rather than a seven. In Fisher's words:

'Among these hundreds of millions of men and women from sixty-two different cultures, individuals speak different languages, ply different trades, wear different clothes, carry different currencies, intone different prayers, fear different devils, and harbour different hopes and different dreams. Nevertheless their divorces regularly cluster around a four year peak.'

She concludes:

'Marriage has a cross-cultural pattern of decay.'

Evidence such as this suggests that divorce could have its roots embedded in evolution.

Attachment styles and divorce

In Chapter 1 we looked at how infant attachment style has been related to later romantic behaviour (see p. 15). Researchers within this area have also applied attachment theory to breakdown, especially divorce. Weiss (1991) suggests that divorce is similar to a death, in so much as an individual will grieve for a 'lost relationship'. Ainsworth (1989) argues that when the sexual interest between couples begins to wane, the care-giving and attachment elements of the relationship become more prominent. Ainsworth argues that romantic relationships at this stage begin to resemble parent–child interactions. Imbalances in this dynamic can contribute towards marital breakdown.

Commentary

Often marriages break up because one partner feels dissatisfied with the level of attention he or she is receiving.

Ainsworth (1989) found that frequently one partner may do most of the giving, and the other most of the taking.

Effects of divorce on children

So far we have been considering divorce in terms of the couple directly involved, but clearly the whole family is affected (Hetherington *et al*,1982). Often children are severely affected. Amato (1991) found that children who had experienced parental separation or divorce showed socio-behavioural problems when interacting with other children. Also, being labelled as a child from a divorced household made the children's lives more difficult. Kitson and Morgan (1990) found that children from divorced families showed higher levels of psychological disturbance (compared to non-divorced families), and often experienced guilt for what was going on inside their home.

Adultery

Kinsey *et al* (1953) found that 50 per cent of American men had engaged in extra-marital affairs compared with 26 per cent of women. In 1980 a poll for *Cosmopolitan* magazine found that 50 per cent of its female readers admitted to having at least one affair. In 1987, sex researcher Shere Hite found that 70 per cent of women married for more than five years had been unfaithful. It appears women are engaging in 'affairs' at probably a similar rate to men.

Explanations of adultery

- Access to other people – modern Western society has provided men and women with vast opportunities to meet new people on a daily basis. The workplace still remains the number one environment for adultery. Buss (1999) argues that our ancient ancestors did not have the opportunities to meet new people. Ancient tribal societies comprised small numbers, making access to 'new people' highly limited. So from this point of view adultery has increased due to increased opportunities.
- Eaker *et al* (1993) suggest that women who are unfaithful are more likely than men to be using an affair as a cry for help. Fisher (1992) argues that from an evolutionary perspective, when a female's mate is no longer perceived as being useful (perhaps because he cannot provide resources, or he has become abusive) it makes sense to seek a new partner.
- Eaker *et al* (1993) identified five types of affairs:
  - The **avoidance-distancing affair**. This is where the adulterer uses an affair to distance himself or herself, or even avoid a relationship that he or she is finding lacking in intimacy. This is particularly common with men.
  - The **peacekeeping affair**. This is an affair whose aim is to assess what is lacking or wrong with a person's 'main relationship'. The adulterer is ironically using it as a desperate attempt to 'rescue' his or her failing existing relationship. Often this type of affair is nothing more than a one-night stand.
  - The **escape hatch**. Many find it difficult to end a relationship, even if they are very unhappy. Often this type of affair gives people a reason to leave. Women tend to engage in this type more than men.
  - **Love-seeking**. Many affairs are based upon flattery. As we saw in Chapter 1, all humans possess a fundamental need to be liked and needed. Often affairs take place when individuals are reaching a crucial milestone in their lives. End-of-decade birthdays are very common times, when people start to feel insecure about their age and their need to feel wanted.
  - **Compulsion**. This is adultery driven by hedonistic urges. Adulterers who fall into this category have little regard for the feelings of others and often engage in affairs for purely sexual reasons. Incidentally, Eaker *et al* found this type represented a small proportion of adulterers.

Jealousy

Apart from love, jealousy is possibly the emotion most frequently associated with relationships. Traditionally, it is perceived in a negative light. Shakespeare described it as 'the green-eyed monster', and *The Song of Solomon* said, 'It's as cruel as the grave'. Studies show that this emotion emerges at a relatively young age. Masciuch and Kienapple (1993) found that very few children showed jealous responses aged eight months; however, by eighteen months most children showed it. Because it appears at such a young age, many scientists have interpreted this as giving it an evolutionary underpinning.

Jealousy from an evolutionary perspective

Mathes (1992) suggested that the most destructive form of jealousy comes from a fear of losing 'sexual exclusivity'. Men are particularly prone to this form of jealousy (Buss *et al*, 1992). Believing that a partner is being unfaithful, or witnessing another man's advances towards his mate can generate the most powerful of jealous responses.

Commentary

In the 1995 trial of O.J. Simpson, prosecutor Darden claimed that Simpson had killed his wife:

'for a reason almost as old as mankind itself ... jealousy – he killed her because he couldn't have her'.

Clearly, the implication was, if she was not interested in him, then Simpson would rather her be dead than show interest in any other man.

Features of jealousy

White and Mullen (1989) described four major stages in the experience of jealousy:

1 **Primary appraisal** – this is where an individual assesses potential threats to the relationship. Melamed (1991) argues that relationships are more prone to jealousy in the early stages when individuals feel more insecure through a lack of knowledge about each other.
2 **Secondary appraisal** – during this stage individuals reassess the situation, and consider ways of dealing with potential threats. Sometimes this can lead to irrational strategies.
3 **Emotional reaction** – during stage two, people have usually generated emotional responses, and it is these which lead to specific behaviours. Most of the time these behaviours are destructive (to either the individuals themselves or the other person). Occasionally, however, jealousy can create positive emotional responses, which can lead to feelings such as excitement and arousal (Pines and Aronson, 1983).
4 **Coping with jealousy** – as we have already pointed out, people cope with jealousy in different ways. In many cases, however, it can lead to feelings of depression and inadequacy (Radecki-Bush *et al*, 1993).

Pathological jealousy

Mowat (1966) compiled an account of jealous murders and concluded that frequently the perpetrators were deluded. They would not respond to rational explanations of events. The responses of the deluded individual were also highly abnormal. Believing their partners to be having affairs they would take their vengeance to extreme levels. Van Sommers (1988) illustrates this point well when he says:

'It is one thing to believe that a partner is meeting a lover in a shed, but another to wait up a tree with a can of petrol and try to incinerate them'.

More recently, an extreme case of jealousy appeared at Cardiff Crown Court which has led some scientists to propose that pathological jealousy has become a modern, major social problem (see RLA 8).

Real Life Application 8:
Jealousy – a pathological condition?

In 1999 Kevin McLaughlin went on trial accused of stabbing his wife 11 times. In every respect he had appeared to be the ideal husband and father of three. The court heard how he had been told that a male colleague of his wife's had smiled at her. This had led him to create a fictitious scenario inside his own mind of his wife's infidelity, which culminated in her murder. He was given a verdict of manslaughter, and sentenced to seven years' imprisonment.

What makes this trial interesting is the verdict. The jury seemed to be influenced by the fact that McLaughlin appeared not to be able to help his behaviour. He was acting on an almost 'irresistible compulsion'. Any other defence and first degree murder would more than likely have been the outcome.

Psychologists in the McLaughlin trial referred to this as a case of 'morbid jealousy' – an overwhelming compulsion to stop his wife from having an affair.

Buss (1999) describes jealousy as a primitive legacy, that ensured our ancestors had some say in who they reproduced with.

De Silva (2000), a psychiatrist based at the Maudsley Hospital, London, claims that there has been a significant increase in patients being referred for therapy for jealousy.

Article adapted from 'Jealousy' by John Cornwell, *The Sunday Times Magazine*, 23 April 2000

Summary

- In 1999 Kevin McLaughlin was convicted of manslaughter – his defence was 'morbid jealousy'.
- Buss (1999) sees jealousy as an adaptive evolutionary mechanism.
- De Silva (2000) has found that cases of jealousy therapy have increased significantly in recent years.

Questions

1 What do you understand by the term 'morbid jealousy'?

2 Give two reasons why cases of jealousy therapy may have increased.

Jealousy and individual differences

Bryson (1991) found many cross-cultural differences in patterns of jealousy. In his study of five countries he found that different nationalities appeared to deal with jealousy in different ways. The French showed the strongest reaction to being betrayed, with those from the Netherlands showing the weakest. American males appeared to favour 'retribution' tactics when they felt their partner was being unfaithful, by flirting or going out with other women. American women, on the other hand, favoured making their partners feel that they didn't care. Italians scored lowest in using social support, when they felt their partners were being unfaithful.

Commentary

Clearly, studies such as Bryson's illustrate both cultural and sex differences in jealousy. However, one point that emerges from most of the work on jealousy is that couples who maintain some of their own independence and self worth, are much more likely to avoid the destruction of the 'green-eyed monster' (Salovey and Rodin, 1988).

An explanation of the Hsitirb tribe (see p. 32)

By reversing the name the society becomes clear. The passage describes a night out at a club using typical 'anthropological language'. Here is a description of the same thing using a more familiar style:

'We like to spend time getting ready before a "night out".

We do our hair, have a shower, apply make-up, perfume or aftershave which we bought in town. It's then time to try on the outfit. Often this requires modification to make yourself look just right. Looking good makes you feel more confident. Once you're at the clubs, cigarettes are smoked, and alcohol drunk. You start dancing, it's hot, crowded and the music's loud and fast. From a distance you see someone you find attractive. This might be your lucky night!'

In 1956, Horace Miner published in the *American anthropologist* an article entitled 'Body ritual among the Nacirema'. It was similar to the article you read on p. 32, except it looked at the Americans. Because it used unfamiliar language (an anthropological style) and it described behaviour out of context, Western readers were made to believe that what they were reading were the rituals of an exotic tribe.

Essay questions

1 Describe and evaluate psychological research into the dissolution (breakdown) of relationships (AEB, Summer 1998).

2 a Outline and evaluate some psychological explanations of the formation of relationships.

b Critically consider how psychologists explain the breakdown of relationships. (AEB, Summer 1997)

3 What have psychologists learnt about the process of attraction?

4 Describe and evaluate the attempts of psychologists to explain the formation and breakdown of friendships.

Intimate relationships

This chapter looks at intimate relationships. It begins by explaining intimate behaviour such as kissing, and touching. It then looks at the concept of love and relationship styles including marriage, monogamy and polygamy. Finally, it explores sexual behaviour including celibacy, heterosexuality, bisexuality and homosexuality and HIV and AIDS. Real Life Applications that are considered are:

- RLA 9: The evolution of kissing
- RLA 10: A Zulu marriage
- RLA 11: Polygamy – a case study
- RLA 12: The 'gay gene'.

Definitions and explanations

'To be intimate means to be close, and I must make it clear at the outset that I am treating this literally.'

So states Desmond Morris at the beginning of his book *Intimate behaviour* (1971). On the face of it, it may appear quite a logical definition. Animals have to get physically close to become intimate. But to what extent is this true in humans? Morris is a zoologist and has for many years advocated studying human behaviour as you would animals. However, some commentators see the link between 'being intimate' and its manifestation as a behaviour as problematic. Humans rationalize emotions to a far greater level of depth than animals. It is our individual interpretation of the intimate behaviour that allows it to be 'truly intimate' (Rycroft, 1985). To clarify this difference between interpretation and actual behaviour, Rycroft cites the example of a kiss.

'For one party to a kiss, it may be a formality or a chore, to the other, an expression of passion or devotion.'

The behaviour is the same in both cases; it is the individual's interpretation of it that can vary.

Commentary

Researchers such as Rycroft (1985) provide a stark warning to psychologists who believe intimacy can be studied from behaviours alone (as in the case of inferring meaning from primates and other animals). Intimacy is an individual experience based upon the love and attachment we have for others.

For the reasons stated above, many psychologists prefer to use a broader definition of the term 'intimate' that makes a distinction between being close in a physical way (in terms of proximity) and being emotionally close to another individual (along the lines of Rycroft's interpretation). The *Oxford English Dictionary* (1981) describes it as:

'having a close acquaintance or friendship with a person'

or

'having a sexual relationship with a person'.

Intimate behaviours

Assuming that both parties involved perceive a specific behaviour to be a gesture of intimacy, there are many actions which could be referred to as intimate. All of them involve body-to-body contact in some form. Desmond Morris in his classic book *Manwatching* (1977) refers to these as 'tie-signs'. Figure 3.1 (p. 53) lists 14 of the most common forms of touch observed and recorded by Morris. Each of them suggests varying degrees of intimacy.

Touch

This topic was looked at in detail in Chapter 1 (see p. 17). However, the focus was from an evolutionary and biological perspective. In this section we will look at touch as an intimate social behaviour.

Proxemics and touch

Proxemics refers to the distances we keep from other people. Hall (1968) suggests we learn 'rules'

- the hand shake
- the body guide
- the pat
- the arm link
- the shoulder embrace
- the full embrace
- the hand-in-hand
- the waist embrace
- the kiss
- the hand-to-head
- the head-to-head
- the caress
- the body support
- the mock attack

Adapted from Desmond Morris,
Manwatching, 1977

Figure 3.1: Human 'tie-signs'

regarding distance, and that these depend upon our culture. Analysing the proximity of couples can often give a good indication of their level of intimacy. Table 3.1 summarizes Hall's categories regarding the distances of 'personal zones'.

Table 3.1: Proxemics, based upon Hall (1968)

Personal zone	Distance	Level of intimacy
Intimate	0–18 inches	Bodily contact – reserved for closest relationships
Personal	18–48 inches	Good friends, but not intimate
Social	48–144 inches	Talking with people at parties or work
Public	144+ inches	Large meetings or lectures

Adapted from Hall (1968)

Commentary

Clearly the distances people are apart when they interact is important. Studies have looked at what happens when these distances are infringed. Felipe and Sommer (1966) found that people were far more likely to leave or erect barriers (such as bags), when a 'stooge' (a confederate of the experimenter) invaded their personal space, by sitting next to them in a library. This was also found to be true, when a stranger sat too close to a participant on a park bench (Sommer, 1969). Having lived in London for a number of years, I frequently witnessed infringements of personal space, while travelling on crowded tube trains. What is fascinating is how quickly

people begin to show how uncomfortable they are feeling. Eye contact with others is avoided and often, even though they are pressed against someone, the head will be turned in a defiant gesture, to make it clear to onlookers there is no intimacy.

The social signals of touch

As we have been stressing so far, the key feature of touch is its signal of intimacy. However, it can convey other signals including warmth and status. A study conducted by Fisher *et al* (1975) found that if librarians touched the hand of readers returning their cards, the readers liked both the librarian and the library better, compared with those who had not been touched. In another study, Henley (1977) found that individuals of higher status touched lower status individuals more (e.g. put an arm around them, etc.).

Commentary

Henley's (1977) study illustrates how easy it is for people in positions of power to abuse their trust, by inappropriately touching their subordinates. A good example of this was the President Clinton and Monica Lewinsky 'liaison'. Lewinsky's lawyers argued she had been a victim of 'sexual intimacy', based upon the status and power of Clinton. However, not all 'status intimate touch' situations lead to abuse. Doctors often have to touch their patients in intimate ways.

Intimate touch within a professional context

One of the most obvious professional groups, where touching is perceived as acceptable is the medical profession. The link between healing and touch has a history as long as the human race itself, and is embedded within all religions. Even today, when medical staff wish to convey a certain level of emotional investment or concern, they touch the patient as a sign of reassurance (McCann and McKerna, 1993). However, the relationship between professionalism and touch is not as clear cut as it might initially appear. People interpret touch in different ways. Mulaik (1991) found that 93 per cent of patients interpreted touch as affection and caring, 74 per cent perceived nurses' touches to be warm, and 77 per cent perceived touch to be about control (the medical staff's status over patients).

Touch and 'courtship behaviour'

In Chapter 2 we looked at the work of David Givens and Timothy Perper (see p. 39). They concluded that successful 'chat-up' strategies progress through five stages. Stage 4 is the 'touching stage' (Givens, 1983; Perper, 1985). These researchers found that normally the woman initiates touching, often by brushing her hand past her suitor's body. Regardless of how insignificant this may appear, by making physical contact the couple have just passed a major barrier, and entered the realms of intimate communication. Clearly, therefore, there must be 'social rules' governing the bodily areas where touching is allowed. We will start by looking at research into taboo areas, then consider cultural variation in touching.

Taboo areas

Jourard (1966) published an interesting article in the *British journal of social and clinical psychology*, in which he identified frequency of bodily touching by relatives and friends (see Figure 3.2). Through this work he identified 'taboo' areas.

Commentary

Desmond Morris (1977), has found even within specific cultures certain body areas are more 'taboo' than others. In Japan the back of a girl's neck is as taboo as touching her breasts. In Thailand, the top of a girl's head is seen as 'untouchable' due to its religious significance.

Sex differences and intimate touching

Nguyen *et al* (1975) questioned male and female undergraduates about their attitudes towards touch. They found that when a close male friend touched a

female in an intimate way, she perceived it to have sexual connotations. However, when the opposite situation occurred males perceived it to represent a wider range of meanings, including love, pleasantness and sexual desire. The researchers concluded that sex differences in touch relate to differences in 'mating strategies'.

Commentary

Studies such as Nguyen *et al*'s raise a number of issues. The work was conducted from a 'heterosexual perspective'. No consideration was made for homosexuality or bisexuality. Also, the links made to 'evolutionary mating strategies' are questionable. The sex differences could be explained by social and cultural learning. Sporting success within teams can often elicit highly 'intimate touching behaviours'. Footballers after scoring a goal are classic examples.

Cultural differences

Even though touch is such a primitive behaviour it is still 'shaped' by social and cultural traditions. A classic cross-cultural study was conducted by Jourard in 1966. He observed couples interacting in coffee shops in different parts of the world. He was particularly interested in how many times couples touched each other during a one-hour period. His results were as follows:

Puerto Rico = 180 times
Paris = 110 times
London = 0 times.

More recently, in the USA, Greenbaum and Rosenfield (1980) carried out a similar study (see Key Study 5).

Desmond Morris (1977) identifies levels of physical contact within different cultural groups. Southern Europe he suggests is, on the whole, less anti-contact than northern Europe. Indeed, Watson and Graves (1966) observed interactions of both Americans and individuals from Arab countries. They found on the whole there was more 'touching' in interpersonal interactions from Arab cultures than American.

Lack of intimate touch

In Chapter 1 we saw how important physical touch (or comfort) is to both human and monkey primates (see RLA 4 on p. 17). It appears touch as an intimate behaviour is vital for our well-being. Studies that have looked at 'sensory deprivation' have shown quite extreme reactions. Bexton *et al* (1954) paid

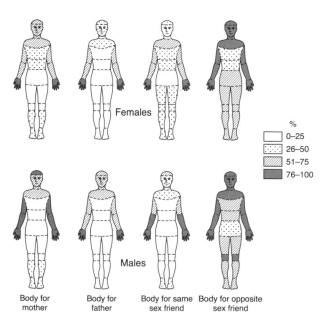

%	
	0–25
	26–50
	51–75
	76–100

Figure 3.2: Frequency of touch by relatives and friends, based upon Jourard (1966)

KEY STUDY 5

Researchers:	Greenbaum and Rosenfield (1980)
Aim:	To assess the frequency of physical contact within a public place.
Method:	A covert observational method was used. 103 interactions were observed at American airports. Greeting responses were recorded.
Results:	Below is a summary of their observations:

No touch at all	41%
Kiss on the mouth	41%
Touch on the head, arm or back	38%
Kiss on cheek	30%
Light hug	23%
Solid hug	19%
Arm round waist or back	15%
Holding hands	12%
Handshake	10%
Extended embrace	10%
Extended kiss	10%

Conclusions:	People appeared to be reluctant to engage in highly intimate behaviours within public places.

American students to take part in a study in which they were isolated from the outside world. They were put in a room without any outside stimulation (no TV, radio, books, etc.). They wore 'frosted glasses', ear muffs and gloves to minimize sensory stimulation. Bexton and colleagues found that the longest any of the participants could tolerate their isolation was three days, the great majority lasted less than 24 hours. Many started to show a variety of mental disturbances, including disorientation, hallucinations and other forms of transient psychosis. Because of studies such as these, most psychologists would agree, sensory isolation can literally cause people to go mad.

Kissing

Kissing is a symbol of intimacy. Kinsey *et al* (1953) found that virtually all Americans had kissed or been kissed. Because it is a form of touch, individuals are 'invading' each other's intimate zones (see proxemics above). Kissing is primarily thought of as a sexual behaviour; however, it does not always convey sexual intentions. Parents kiss their children, heterosexual friends may kiss one another, purely as a sign of affection, political leaders (of certain countries) may kiss and embrace, as a sign of respect and unity. So where does this 'primitive' behaviour originate?

The evolution of the kiss

Some anthropologists believe that kissing originated in the act of passing pre-chewed food to weaning infants (incidentally a behaviour still practized in some tribal cultures today). It is argued that the roots of 'deep tongue kissing' (a behaviour found primarily in sexual relationships) can be traced back to the primitive searching movements of an infant's tongue inside its mother's mouth (Morris, 1977). However, scientists have proposed a number of hypotheses regarding the origins of kissing (see RLA 9).

Real Life Application 9:
The evolution of kissing

Listed below is a selection of explanations as to the origins and effects of kissing.

- As mentioned above it relates back to kiss-feeding – the process by which mothers chewed solid food into a 'mush', then fed it back, mouth-to-mouth to their offspring (Morris, 1977).

- It gives 'pleasurable sensations', which become addictive – Harter (1999) points out that five out of the twelve cranial nerves are involved in kissing. Also, providing the kissers both consent, changes in bio-chemistry ensue, immediately after the kiss has begun. Levels of dopamine (a feel-good neurotransmitter) begin to rise, so too does testosterone, and adrenaline and noradrenaline. This causes the heartbeat to increase from, on average, 60–80 beats per minute, to beyond 100. During especially passionate kissing, the hormone oxytocin is secreted. It is believed that this hormone is involved in us feeling the need for closeness (see Chapter 1, p. 13 for more details).

- Another possible hypothesis is that kissing was a way of 'tasting' your potential mate. Secretions of sebum from the glands near the lips were a way of testing sexual chemistry. It could also be a way of testing for pheromones (see Chapter 1, p. 10).

- Both chimpanzees and pygmy chimps (bonobos) regularly engage in kissing, even using their tongues. This suggests that kissing pre-dates humans, or it evolved independently after our evolutionary lines diverged.

- Another hypothesis suggests that kissing is an 'adult' extension of suckling behaviour in babyhood. Nick Fisher, author of *A complete guide to kissing*, points out:

  'Without this type of sucking kiss you'd go hungry and feel unloved.'

  Therefore the links between infantile behaviour and adult sexual behaviour is based upon the comfort and security we experienced when we were totally dependent infants. This regressive behaviour hypothesis is a theme Freud identified within his theory of psychosexual development. He proposed that the first stage a neonate (newborn) goes through, confers erotic energy (libido) upon the mouth and associated areas. This is referred to as the oral phase (Freud, 1905). During this stage the newborn experiences 'sexual' pleasure from indulging in the sucking reflex. Freud proposed the primary source of this behaviour was in breastfeeding. Any anxiety experienced during this stage leads to 'oral fixations' later in life. Any adult behaviour that involves touching the mouth could be classed as orally fixated behaviour. When we are anxious it is a natural human response to reach for our mouths. Smoking and nail biting are two examples of this. In a Freudian sense kissing could be regarded as 'regressive infantile sucking behaviour' that is driven by a need to feel secure.

- Is kissing unhealthy? In our Westernized society, we have become obsessed with hygiene. Bacteria, viruses, even meningitis are all infections which can be spread by water droplet contamination. However, Weinberg (1999), consultant epidemiologist based at the Pubic Health Laboratory Service in London, points out that most of the 'bugs' in our mouths are beneficial, or at worst harmless. In fact, he goes on to suggest that exchanging these 'bugs' through passing saliva to one another (through kissing) could be 'essential to our survival'.

Article adapted from 'Lips Wide Shut' by Tony Barrell, *The Sunday Times* Magazine, 17 October 1999

Summary

- One explanation of kissing suggests it originates in kiss-feeding.
- We engage in kissing because it alters our physiology, making us 'feel good'.
- Another explanation of kissing is that we need to taste our potential partner. This could be a similar mechanism to pheromones.
- Kissing could be seen as an extension of 'baby suckling behaviour'.
- Kissing could provide an exchange of useful 'oral bacteria' which could have been vital in our survival (Weinberg, 1999).

Questions

1 What social benefits might there be in kissing?

2 What are the drawbacks of viewing kissing as an 'adaptive evolutionary' behaviour?

Cultural variations

Kissing in its Western form is not a culturally universal behaviour. Some Innuit and Truk Islander societies rub their noses together rather than kiss. Other cultures including the Kwakiutl Indians and the Trobriand Islanders engage in a form of kissing which involves sucking the lips and tongue (Diamond, 1992). In extreme cases, rather than kissing, the mouth is used to inflict pain as part of the sexual technique. The Apinaye women of South America may bite off bits of their partner's eyebrows, noisily spitting them aside. In many tribal cultures, biting to the point of drawing blood is common (Ford and Beach, 1951).

Commentary

Behaviours such as touching and kissing indicate intimacy. However, the 'outward manifestations' of these behaviours are not the same in every culture.

We now turn our attention to the underlying emotion of intimacy, namely love.

Love

Love is possibly, the most talked about, written about and sung about, of all human experiences. A Harris research poll in 1991 showed that, at any one time, one in ten people in Britain described themselves as being madly in love. Only 20 per cent of people questioned said that they were not in love. If these figures were extrapolated to the population as a whole, we would have a lot of people being 'in love' to some extent. Despite love being such a widely held emotion, it has only been in recent years that scientists have involved themselves in unravelling its mysteries. Maslow (1954) pointed out:

'It is amazing how little the empirical sciences have to offer on the subject of love.'

Why has this been the case? Some commentators such as Burgess and Wallin (1953) believe there are two main reasons. Firstly, it wasn't until the middle part of the twentieth century that scientists actually 'believed' that love was amenable to empirical study. Prior to this it had always been within the domain of poets, philosophers and theologians. Secondly, people's attitudes towards love and sexuality had always been much more reserved, making past research in this field taboo.

Types of love

The Ancient Greeks believed there were different types of love, depending upon the person and the situation. The sociologist J.A. Lee (1973) identified six 'styles' of loving based upon the Greek terms:

- Ludus – game-playing love
- Mania – possessive love
- Pragma – logical love
- Agape – selfless (altruistic) love
- Storage – companionate love
- Eros – erotic love.

Hendrick and Hendrick (1986) took this idea further by looking at sex differences between the dif-

Table 3.2: Attitudes towards different styles of love, based upon Hendrick and Hendrick (1986)

Love type	Description	Sex difference
Game playing	Treating love like a game or competition	Men more than women
Possessive	Psychologically trying to 'tie the partner down'	Women more than men
Logical	Treating love as a rational process	Women more than men
Altruistic	Putting the other person first	No difference found
Companionate	Developing a close, meaningful friendship	Women slightly more than men
Erotic	Sexual pleasure	No difference found

ferent types of love. They studied attitudes towards the different 'love styles' in America during the mid-1980s. Table 3.2 summarizes their findings.

Commentary

There have been a number of cross-cultural studies which have looked at the prevalence of the 'love styles'. For example, Goodwin and Findlay (1997) found that Hong Kong Chinese students engaged in more logical and altruistic forms of love than their British counterparts. It appears that different cultures show preferences for different 'types' of love, and this would be shaped by socialization.

Companionate and passionate (romantic) love

Hatfield (1988) made a distinction between companionate love and passionate love. Companionate love is what we feel for those who share our life in a significant way. These could include marriage partners and close friends. It is marked by mutual concern of the welfare of the other person (Hendrick and Hendrick, 1986). Passionate love is reserved for very special people, and was defined as:

'a state of intense absorption in another'.

The explanation goes on to point out that companionate love produces:

'a state of intense physiological arousal'.

Passionate love

More than any other type, passionate (or romantic) love has been the one that has puzzled commentators since the dawn of humankind. Not only does it defy logic, but it becomes a roller coaster ride of emotions, throwing normally sane individuals into the realms of obsession and delusion. For example, you would think that experiencing difficulties within a relationship would dampen down the flames of passion. However, studies have shown the opposite effect. Difficulties can actually increase passion (Hindy et al, 1989). Hollywood films often use this phenomenon to create aggression one minute and passion the next, within the relationships between the leading actors. So how do biology and psychology work together to produce such an 'inflammable' behaviour? In 1974, Berscheid and Walster proposed an interesting hypothesis. They based it upon Schacter and Singer's (1964), two-factor theory of emotion (see Figure 3.3). They suggested that passionate love consists of two components: (1) physiological arousal, and (2) a belief that

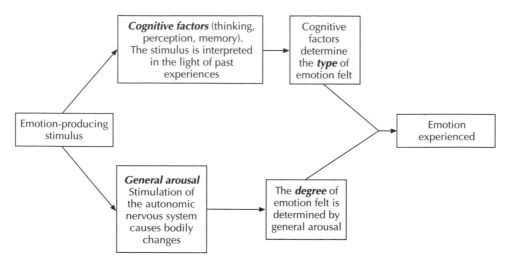

Figure 3.3: Schacter and Singer's (1964) two-factor theory of emotion

this arousal is caused by the presence of the 'beloved'. Now clearly, on some occasions we are very much aware that the presence of someone is causing arousal. But there are times when arousal can be misattributed.

Excitation transfer

Dolf Zillman (1984) calls the process of misattribution 'excitation transfer'. An individual interprets 'powerful emotions' as love, when in actual fact they are something else. What other emotions could be misinterpreted? The Roman scholar Ovid in his book *The art of love* suggests that men should take potential female partners to watch the gladiators fight, where 'she could be easily aroused to passion'. Perhaps not an ideal date for couples today, but psychologists now understand why it must have worked for the Romans. A classic case of 'excitation transfer'. Fear was being misattributed for sexual passion.

Commentary

The nursing times of 10 February 2000 carried an article with the headline 'Affairs at work – when stress and trauma lead to romance'. As the title implies, working in stressful and traumatic situations can lead to an increase in workplace affairs. The article looked at case studies of nurses who have been drawn into having affairs at work. Another classic case of 'excitation transfer' was described by one nurse who said:

'When you share an intense experience you can feel a very deep attraction.'

Psychological studies into the 'excitation transfer effect'

Over the years a number of psychological studies have been conducted which have given weight to the concept of 'excitation transfer'. A classic study was conducted by Dutton and Aron in 1974 (see Key Study 6).

Commentary

There are a number of flaws in this study;

- Perhaps only certain men would attempt to cross the higher suspension bridge – more 'risk-taking', 'macho' individuals, who were more socially outgoing. This would of course explain the differences, not the excitation transfer effect.
- Perhaps the female interviewer acted differently on the higher bridge than the lower one.
- Some researchers have suggested that it may be comforting to be with someone when we're feeling distressed. Rather than sexual arousal, it could have been relief that the men experienced (Kendrick and Cialdini, 1977).

In 1981, White *et al* set up a further study to test excitation transfer. However, this time, they wanted to rule out the possibility that fear was creating the misattribution, rather than just generalized arousal. So, rather than exposing male participants to distressful stimuli (as in the case of the suspension bridge), they induced arousal by getting the participants to 'run on the spot', for either two minutes or fifteen seconds. They then showed the men a video of a woman they expected to meet later. The female was a confederate of the researcher, and was made

KEY STUDY 6

Researchers: Dutton and Aron (1974)

Aim: The aim of the study was to see if male participants would attribute their high arousal to being in the presence of a female, rather than walking across a high suspension bridge.

Method: The participants were unsuspecting males aged 18–35, who were visiting the Capilano Canyon in British Columbia, Canada. The experiment took place on two of the bridges at this popular tourist spot. The first one is 450 feet long, 5 feet wide, and it swings precariously, 230 feet above a rocky gorge. This, not surprisingly, the researchers termed the 'high arousal condition'. The second bridge is much lower, only 10 feet above the ground. It is very stable and this was termed the 'low arousal condition'. Whenever an unaccompanied young man walked across either of the bridges he was met half way across and interviewed by an attractive male or female researcher. The respondent answered a few questions (actually designed to detect sexual imagery), then he was given a telephone number and asked to phone if he wanted any further information regarding the study.

Results: What was found was that four times as many men called from the high arousal condition, than the low. Also, more sexual imagery was identified during the 'high arousal interviews'.

Conclusions: The male participants appeared to have attributed their high state of arousal to the female interviewer, rather than the precarious suspension bridge.

up either to look attractive or plain. What was found was that those men who had exercised for two minutes rated the female in the attractive condition as more attractive, and in the plain condition as less attractive, when compared to the men who exercised for only fifteen seconds. It appeared the increased arousal (due to increased exercise) encouraged more extreme ratings.

Commentary

Work such as White *et al*'s suggests that misattribution is not directly related to fear or distress (as was originally thought by Ovid, and Dutton and Aron (1974)), but by the general physiological arousal of the individual.

The bio-chemistry of passion

More recently, psychologists have started to look directly at the bio-chemistry of passion. In 1983, Liebowitz suggested that the physiological changes associated with passionate love were comparable with the effects of stimulant drugs such as amphetamines. In another study Professor Semir Zeki and colleagues (2000), at University College, London, scanned the brains of volunteers who had described themselves as being 'truly and madly' in love. They found that when the participants were shown pictures of their loved ones, certain regions of the brain became more active. Table 3.3 summarizes the areas that were activated, and describes their function and possible relevance to being 'madly in love'.

Triangular theory of love

Another theorist to develop a framework for analysing types of love was Robert Sternberg (1986). He referred to it as the triangular theory of love. It comprises three components (see Figure

Table 3.3: Brain structures and their association to being in love, based upon Zeki (2000)

Brain structure	Function/symptom of being in love
Medial insula	Links together all the sensory areas of the brain. This might explain 'unusual bodily sensations' often reported by lovers
Anterior cingulate	This area is associated with 'euphoria inducing' drugs. This could explain the 'high' experienced by people in love. It might also explain being 'lovesick' – its withdrawal symptoms
Parts of the basal ganglia	This a 'primitive' area of the brain associated with rewarding experiences and addiction. This may suggest we could get 'hooked on' being madly in love

3.4). It stresses the dynamic nature of love – how it can change as time passes.

Figure 3.4 illustrates the different types of loving and how the characteristics change, shifting the centre of gravity within the triangle (Gilmour, 1988). An individual in their twenties has 'their triangle' weighed heavily towards passion, with some weighting on intimacy and the least on commitment. However, over the years things change and by the time that person is in their forties, passion has decreased considerably, intimacy has increased slightly and commitment has increased greatly. In this case, the relationship started off as a passionate attraction, and ended up as a more practical love (high on commitment).

Commentary

Sternberg's model illustrates that the three different types of love vary over time. Often the qualities of love which are important at one stage of an individual's life may not be so important at another. Research shows that out of the three types, commitment is the best predictor of relationship endurance and satisfaction (Whitley, 1993). More recently, some academics have questioned whether intimacy is a separate component within the model (Acker and Davis, 1992). Clearly, this has impli-

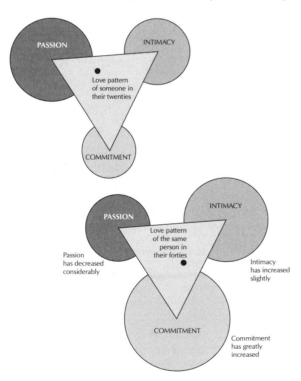

Figure 3.4: The triangular theory of love, based upon Sternberg. From Psychological Review, 1986, 93, 119–135. Copyright © 1986 by the American Psychological Association. Reprinted with permission.

cations, as there would no longer be a triangle. All that would be left is passion and commitment, which ironically resemble Hatfield's (1988) original distinctions (passion and companionate love).

Marriage

It is usual within nearly all cultures for couples to demonstrate publicly their commitment to one another by getting married. The Office for National Statistics (1997) shows:

- most young people expect to marry (over 70 per cent)
- the majority of British marriages still involve a bride and a groom
- women tend to marry men older than themselves.

We will see later in this chapter, and in Chapter 4, that many commentators refer to 'family values'. The basis of family life is a married couple. Indeed, by making marriage 'the norm', society encourages both 'pair-bonding' (monogamy) and heterosexuality (Rich, 1980).

Same-sex marriages

Even though same-sex marriages are not fully recognized by law in Great Britain, in October 1999 a judge passed a ruling that a homosexual couple living in a stable relationship could be defined as 'a family'. Many homosexual couples who are in stable long-term relationships create ceremonies of their own. Often they exchange wedding rings and set up joint mortgages and bank accounts, in the same way as heterosexual couples would. It has only been in recent years that researchers have started to look at 'gay marriage' as distinct from 'straight'. It was always assumed that gay relationships would be conducted in the same way as heterosexual. One obvious area of difference is related to gender roles in the 'domestic division of labour'. Rather than being influenced by media portrayals of what men and women should do in the home, partners in gay marriages have to 'negotiate their own relationship rules' (Yip, 1999). In one interview of a gay couple, one partner said:

'I am better at the maintenance of the house, so I will do the washing-up, ironing, cleaning and whatever … he is more a project person' (Yip, 1997).

Commentary

By studying same-sex 'marriages', psychologists are able to look at the effects of 'social control' and its influence on intimate relationships. Many gay couples argue that they feel excluded by the majority of society. Partners have to be careful how they appear in public places (kissing, holding hands, etc.). So, on the one hand, gay 'marriages' are restrictive, but on another they are liberating because there is no 'formalized social script' which they have to conform to, as many heterosexual married couples do (Yip, 1999).

The psychology and sociology of marriage

Apart from the obvious benefits of being married (such as companionship, a stable sexual relationship, a sense of being wanted by someone else, etc.), psychologists and sociologists over the years have developed models and theories which attempt to explain the purpose and function of marriage.

Sex differences regarding marriage

Sex roles within marriage are changing. The stereotype of the wife doing the housework and cooking the tea, while her husband goes out to work has changed. In spring 1998, 60 per cent of married women with pre-school age children were economically active (this means earning money in one way or another) (*Social Trends*, 1999). In line with this it appears that women's attitudes towards marriage have changed also. Women look for greater equality and autonomy within their marriages (Sharpe, 1994). During the 1980s, Mansfield and Collard undertook a study which assessed sex differences in attitudes towards the objectives of marriage. It appeared that men wanted physical and emotional security – a secure base to come home to, whereas women wanted 'close intimacy', and a feeling of being wanted as a person rather than just a wife (Mansfield and Collard, 1988).

Commentary

Evidence such as this suggests that men and women go into relationships looking for, and requiring, different things. However, all is not lost, as marriage therapist, and author of *Men are from Mars, women are from Venus*, Jon Gray (1994) puts it:

'When men and women are able to respect and accept their differences, then love has a chance to blossom.'

So how can these differences begin to be understood? One way is to look at how couples attribute blame and other events within their marriage.

Marriage and attributional style

Many psychologists have attempted to explain how married couples assess one another's behaviour. As we have seen above, it is hoped that a better understanding of attributions can lead to more enriched and successful relationships. Bradbury and Fincham (1990) looked at the attributions that married couples made regarding their relationships. They found these related to the 'success' or level of happiness of that marriage. There are three dimensions upon which attributions can be made:

- external versus internal
- stable versus unstable
- global versus specific.

These six descriptions can be defined in the following ways:

- External – caused by some 'outside factor', may be the environment or another person.
- Internal – caused by the individual themselves, something intrinsic to them.
- Stable – this situation isn't going to go away.
- Unstable – this situation is only temporary.
- Global – this situation seems to affect everything in your life.
- Specific – this situation is limited.

Let us now consider two fictitious examples to illustrate how this theory might be applied.

John and Linda have just had an argument. Linda has accused John of looking at other women at a party they have just been to. John has just accused Linda of being too paranoid.

Linda is attributing in the following way:

- Internal – John has some sort of insecure personality problem, that's why he wants other women to take notice of him.
- Stable – this problem he has is not going away.
- Global – it isn't just at the party that John does this, it's every time they socialize.

Mike and Fiona have just had an argument. Mike has had to wait half an hour for Fiona to come home from shopping, and it has made him late for an appointment.

Mike is attributing in the following way:

- External – Fiona must have got held up in traffic.
- Unstable – she is normally so punctual.
- Specific – she normally helps with other areas of my business.

Bradbury and Fincham (1990) suggest happy couples minimize the 'bad' by making external, unstable and specific attributions (as in the case of example 2 above), and maximize the 'good' by making internal, stable and global attributions (see Figure 3.5). They go on to suggest that unhappy couples do the opposite. They maximize the 'bad' by making internal, stable and global attributions (as in the case of example 1 above) and they minimize the 'good' by making external, unstable and specific attributions (see Figure 3.6).

Commentary

Explanations such as those proposed by Bradbury and Fincham (1990) are useful in assessing the 'potential success' of relationships. Indeed, Fincham and Bradbury (1993) found that couples who made more 'distress maintaining' attributions (see Figure 3.6) reported less marital satisfaction a year later. However, as Fincham and Bradbury point out, this correlation between attri-

butions and satisfaction could be reciprocal. It could be that general marital dissatisfaction leads to 'distress maintaining attributions'. Whichever way around it is, it does not detract from the theory's applicability to real life.

Being married is good for your health

We already found in Chapter 1 that the quality of an individual's relationships can have an impact upon his or her physical and psychological health (see p. 19). Most of the research literature has compared the health of married couples with separated or divorced individuals. We will now consider some of this evidence:

• Kiecolt-Glaser and Glaser (1986) found that separated and divorced women had impaired

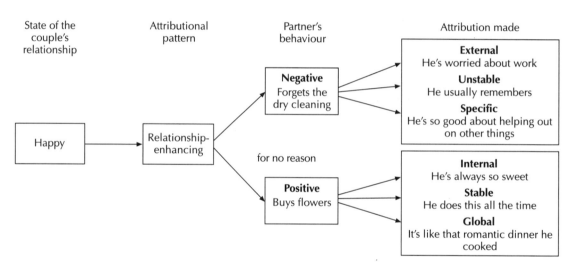

Figure 3.5: The attributions of happy couples, based upon Bradbury and Fincham (1990)

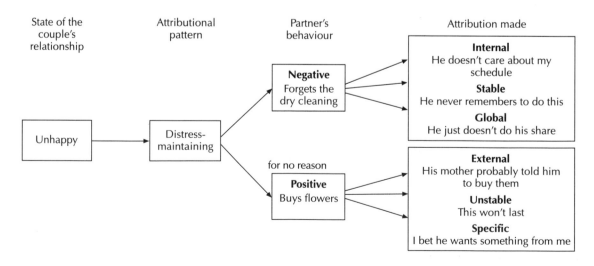

Figure 3.6: The attributions of unhappy couples, based upon Bradbury and Fincham (1990)

immune system functioning, compared to a matched control group.

- Lynch (1977) found that married people were much less likely to die from a variety of physical illnesses, than single, separated or divorced people of the same age. Incidentally, this effect appeared stronger for men than women.
- Kurdeck (1989) found that men suffer more from the death of a spouse or marital disruption than women.
- Cochrane (1988) found that the rates of admissions to mental hospitals were significantly less for married individuals than single, widowed or divorced.
- Being married appears also to have a 'knock-on effect' to offspring as well. Studies have shown that infant low birth weight is more common for children of unmarried women than their married counterparts (Power, 1995).

Commentary

The studies listed above illustrate a number of points regarding health and marriage:

- Being married appears to 'act as a buffer' against ill health.
- Men appear to benefit slightly more than women from this fact.
- Research such as Power's shows that even offspring can benefit from their parents being married.

However, we must be careful not to assume that it is the marriage itself that is responsible for these benefits. It could be that, for some reason, healthier individuals are more successful at 'keeping marriages together'.

Sociologists Berger and Kellner (1964) argued that marriage allows individuals to make sense of the world, through their interactions as a couple. When couples marry (because they have come from different homes, different family backgrounds, etc.), they have to develop a new reality of shared interests and common goals. This might explain why many families become quite nepotistic and inward looking.

Clark (1991) carried out interviews on young couples, in Aberdeen, shortly after they had got married. He found that he could distinguish four types of marriage:

1 Drifting – the couples had uncertainties about the future.
2 Surfacing – in this group at least one of the partners had been married before. Problems relating to the previous relationship kept intruding on the current one.

3 Establishing – the couples had plans for the future and worked together.
4 Struggling – most of these couples had financial difficulties. This put a strain on their personal relationships.

Commentary

Ideas such as Berger and Kellner's and Clark's are useful in identifying the social role marriage has. Marriage allows people to become 'identified' within society. Whether the identification that is made is acceptable or not depends primarily upon the accepted norms of any given culture.

Cultural differences in marriage

As mentioned earlier, marriage in one form or another appears to be found in all cultures. However, the structure, attitudes and values attached to it vary. Let us now consider some of these variations.

The 'Nayar' of northern India are a good example of cultural variation to marriage from a modern Western perspective (Schneider and Gough, 1972):

- The women of the tribe were seen to 'carry' the ancestral line from a common ancestress (the Taravad).
- A child becomes a member of the mother's Taravad, not the father's.
- Girls went through a ceremony before puberty which would roughly equate to a 'marriage'. However, they would then be permitted to take as many lovers as they wished.
- Husbands and fathers were entirely peripheral to the domestic life of their wives and children.

Another interesting variation was described by the anthropologist Evans-Pritchard (1951) as a 'ghost marriage'. One society where this frequently occurs is the 'Nuer' people of the Nile Basin. When a male dies either unmarried or without children, a close kinsman (related to him through his father's line) will marry and any children born of this union will be seen as the 'dead man's' children. This process may continue again and again.

The Zulu people of South Africa engage in a long, serious period of courtship prior to marriage. As with many tribal cultures, marriage is seen as a business negotiation. However, unlike some of the tribal cultures outlined above, the process of 'boy meets girl' doesn't appear that dissimilar to modern Western traditions (see RLA 10).

Real Life Application 10:
A Zulu marriage

When a Zulu man prepares to marry, there are certain rules and etiquette that must be observed. The process follows a series of stages.

The love affair

'Senior girls' (older girls given positions of authority) decide for younger girls if they are ready for a boyfriend. Their consent (not the parents') is required for the relationship to start. The male then requires a confession of love from the girl, which she must say to his face. The senior girl (the one who is overseeing the whole process) then grants permission for the practice of 'hlobonga' to begin. This is where the couple spend evenings and nights together, however sexual intercourse is forbidden. The man is required to get the girl home before sunrise, otherwise he must pay a penalty of a goat to her father.

The 'courting hut'

Even though the girl's father denies all knowledge of hlobonga, and officially forbids any potential suitors to his home, he builds a special hut for them to meet in. This rather bizarre situation is an example of the subtleness of courtship behaviour within Zulu culture, and illustrates the power of etiquette (Elliott, 1978).

Engagement procedures

Eventually, the father acknowledges his daughter's suitor, by asking her to 'fetch some cattle from her lover'. This marks the start of 'lobola'.

Lobola negotiations

In the late 1970s, ten plus one head of cattle was the lobola for a virgin. The one, ironically, is to compensate her mother for losing her daughter. Zulu men often marry in their early twenties, so they are not wealthy enough to pay the lobola. In these situations it is customary for fathers and brothers to help out.

The marriage ceremony

Eventually after lobola, a date is set for the wedding ceremony itself. On the morning of the wedding, the bride spends the morning at the river where she and her handmaidens spend their time bathing naked. At the ceremony itself, relations from both sides of the family form lines which literally oppose each other. Once the ceremony is underway these lines disperse and the two families mix. The ceremony can often go on for two or three days, with plenty of eating and drinking.

Article adapted from Aubrey Elliott, 'Sons of Zulu', Collins, 1978

Summary

- Zulu marriages follow certain rules and etiquette.
- There are five main stages to Zulu courtship. In nearly every case it leads to marriage.
- As with many tribal marriages it involves negotiations using animals.

As we have seen above, marriage can be 'defined' in many ways. Social scientists tend to use two main categories when defining 'types of marriage', namely monogamy and polygamy. Let us look at these in turn.

Questions

1 What role does love play in a Zulu marriage?

2 In what ways do the stages of a Zulu marriage parallel a modern Western one?

Monogamy

The Western model of marriage is based upon monogamy. This is where an individual has one sexual partner at a time. It is illegal in British law for a man or woman to be married to more than one individual at any one time. Anyone who breaks this law is referred to as a 'bigamist'.

Polygamy

This describes marriages where more than one sexual partner is permitted or encouraged at any one time. The assumption that monogamy is the norm in every culture was refuted by Murdock (1949). He found that polygamy was reported in 80 per cent of societies he studied. There are two types of polygamy:

- polygyny – this is where a man may be married to more than one woman at the same time.
- polyandry – this is where a woman may be married to more than one man at the same time. This marriage style is much less common.

Commentary

What are the psychological implications of the three marriage types? Monogamy is conducive to what we have learnt about, in terms of fulfilling a psychological need. A one-to-one union is intimate, brings close attachment and makes individuals feel special (raises self-esteem). Polygamy on the other hand exemplifies 'an evolutionary imperative', namely, it increases the likelihood of reproduction through sexual variation. However, many cultures (including Britain) still view polygamy as a 'moral impediment' (see RLA 11).

Real Life Application 11:

Polygamy – a case study

Muslims in Britain are to challenge British law which forbids a husband from having more than one wife. In Islamic law men are able to have up to four wives. However, this is not for sexual gratification. The law is only invoked if the man's first wife is infertile, or if she is considered to be a social outcast. There are no official figures on the number of people practising polygamy in Britain, however estimations suggest it could be hundreds.

One British Muslim woman suffering as a result of polygamy is Sameera, whose 55-year-old husband obtained a second wife while on holiday in Pakistan. In actual fact it was his 26-year-old cousin. Sameera was devastated when she heard the news:

'I just fainted when I first heard,' said Sameera. 'The fact he has married such a young girl, a girl old enough to be his daughter.'

Noshaba Hussein from the Muslim Parliament says she knows of many happy polygamous marriages in Britain.

'I am aware that this practice is taking place in Britain, and there are couples who are quite happy and satisfied with their relationship and they would like to carry on and be protected by law.'

However, not everyone holds this view. The Bishop of Rochester, Dr Nazir Ali said:

'I don't think that polygamy should be enshrined in law because it will affect the mutual love and companionship that a marriage needs and it will also affect the stability of the family.'

Article adapted from BBC News on Yahoo (www.uknews.yahoo.com),18 June 2000

Summary

- Polygamy is illegal in Britain. However, Muslims in Britain are set to challenge this law.
- Islamic law permits a man to take up to four wives.
- Noshaba Hussein from the Muslim Parliament argues there are many polygamous marriages in Britain, and that the people involved are quite happy about the arrangements.
- Dr Nazir Ali, the Bishop of Rochester, warns that legalizing polygamy will adversely affect mutual love and companionship and have effects upon family life.

Questions

1 To what extent do you feel polygamy is a 'social construct'?

2 Identify some of the 'pros and cons' of polygamy.

Sexual relationships

Intimacy must not be regarded as a euphemism for sex. As we saw earlier, intimacy may be found between best friends (platonic) and between parents and children. However, lovers also show intimacy through the development of 'sexual relationships'. It is types of sexual relationships that will be considered next.

Abstinence

This can be defined as a total 'lack of sexual behaviour'. It can relate to pre-marital sex or sexual behaviour in general (as in the case of religious hermits). Gallup polls conducted in America from the 1960s show an increasingly positive attitude towards pre-marital sex. Table 3.4 summarizes these findings.

Table 3.4: A comparison of American Gallup polls (1969–87) showing the percentage of respondents who viewed sex before marriage as 'wrong'

Do you think it is wrong for a man and woman to have relations before marriage or not?	1969	1978	1987
Yes, it is wrong	68%	50%	46%
No, it is not wrong	21%	41%	48%
Don't know	11%	9%	6%

Commentary

Table 3.4 raises a number of interesting points. Firstly, the percentage of people who think 'sex before marriage' is wrong decreased from 68 per cent (in 1969) to 46 per cent (in 1987). However, over 18 years this is only a decrease of 22 per cent. This reflects that American social attitudes even in the late 1980s were still quite moralistic. Secondly, the number of people who were unable to answer the question also decreased over the years. This could indicate that attitudes towards 'sex questionnaires' have become less taboo.

Many religions (including Catholicism) have developed strict rules regarding sexuality. Roman Catholic priests are forbidden to marry, and have to take a 'vow of celibacy'. However, congregations are also expected to engage in 'self control'. In 1983 the Vatican issued 'Educational guidance in human love', a pamphlet for parents and teachers. It proposed masturbation, extra-marital sex and homosexuality were 'grave moral disorders'. It argued the only 'ethical sexuality' is that which leads to procreation. However, some religions such as Hinduism stress both abstinence and sexuality. Hinduism states that 'brahmacarya' (or celibacy) should be cultivated at the beginning of life (when an individual should be studying), and at the end of life (when an individual should be contemplating wisdom). In between, it is possible to marry and raise a family. Active sexuality and asceticism (severe self-discipline) are possible within the same lifetime (Noss, 1963).

Heterosexuality

A heterosexual is an individual whose sexual preference is for a member of the opposite sex. As we saw in Chapter 1, many researchers regard this sexuality as the 'norm', because of its obvious benefits for reproduction.

Bisexuality

A bisexual is an individual whose sexual orientation is towards both men and women. Some scientists refer to this as being ambisexual. Bisexuality has become quite a 'trendy' behaviour, particularly in many American large cities where so-called 'bi-bars' have opened up. However, many homosexuals view bisexuality with suspicion or outright hostility (Blumstein and Schartz, 1976). Radical lesbians in particular see bisexual women as betraying the lesbian cause, because they enjoy having sex with men.

Homosexuality

A definition

The term 'homosexual' was coined in the 1850s by Benkart, a doctor from Leipzig in Germany. It derives from the Greek 'homo' meaning same and not, as many believe, the Latin 'homo' meaning man. It describes individuals who are sexually attracted to members of their own sex. Today the word 'gay' is more commonly used, although many female homosexuals prefer the term 'lesbianism' (Mills, 1993).

A history of homosexuality

The Ancient Greeks did not view sexuality in the same way as modern Western society. Plato, when describing the sexual behaviour of Iccus of Tarentum, suggested that he was able to abstain from relations with boys and women alike. In fact, young boys having sexual relations with other boys in their youth, then later showing preferences for women was very common in Greek society (Foucault, 1984). Does this mean that all Greeks were bisexual? Foucault goes on to suggest that in modern 'Western eyes' they were because we distinguish between the two types of attraction (same sex and different sex), however …

'To their way of thinking what made it possible to desire a man or a woman was simply the appetite that nature had implanted in man's heart for "beautiful" human beings whatever their sex might be' (Foucault 1984).

According to Boswell (1980), it was the Roman emperor Justinian who decreed that homosexuality should be punishable by death. The early thirteenth century saw homosexual acts being described as the 'the crime not fit to be named'. Eighteenth-century Europe saw sexual relationships between men as perverted. The act of sodomy (anal sex) was seen by the Church as unnatural, and its non-procreative aspects were stressed. In 1761 a young homosexual man of London, who had been sentenced for attempted buggery, was almost lynched by the awaiting crowd, such was the homophobia of this time. In fact, two years later two homosexuals were killed by onlookers (Wagner, 1988). The term 'sodomites' was used to describe homosexuals, and being accused of being a 'sodomite' carried a severe social stigma. Ironically, lesbianism appears to have been tolerated far more. Homophobia in eighteenth-century England focused on men. Their behaviour seemed to threaten the independence and aggression traditionally associated with the male (MacCormack and Stathern, 1980).

In 1895 the author and dramatist Oscar Wilde was accused of 'gross indecency' and despite a highly articulate defence of homosexual love, he was sent to Reading jail for two years. It was another 72 years before homosexuality was decriminalized in England.

Frequency in the population

According to one of the most comprehensive reports conducted during the 1940s in America (Kinsey *et al*,1948), 4 per cent of American men were exclusively homosexual. The figure was 2 per cent among women (Kinsey *et al*, 1953). Even today homosexuality is viewed as being statistically infrequent. According to figures collected for the government's General Household Survey, only 0.0014 per cent of the population lives in a homosexual household (1997). Statisticians had planned to include the number of 'gay households' but found them to be too few. On the basis of surveys such as these it has been estimated that fewer than 100,000 out of a population of 58.4 million are living in stable homosexual relationships. However, gay pressure groups such as Stonewall Lobby Group Ltd have frequently claimed that one in ten of the population is gay.

There has been very little in the way of reliable research into the incidence of lesbianism. However, it is estimated that one in 50 women are exclusively lesbian and about the same occasionally or in fantasy (Diamond, 1992).

Commentary

Look at the issue of which source is right.

The gay question was 'Are you living together as a couple?'. Haskey (1997) from the Office for National Statistics said:

'It was a pretty neutral question. People know what it means, they don't misinterpret it.'

Male homosexuality and the law

British law divides homosexuality for males into two offences. The first is 'buggery or sodomy' (anal sex), which is also a heterosexual offence. The second is 'gross indecency between males'. However, the Sexual Offences Act 1967 states that 'gay sex' between consenting adults is not a criminal offence. However, there are three conditions placed on this:

- The age of consent is 18 (this was reduced from 21 in 1994).

- Homosexual sex must take place within a private dwelling (in other words, behind 'closed doors').
- It is unlawful if there are more than two people present.

Commentary

In 1995 there were nearly 500 prosecutions for gross indecency. Nearly 90 per cent of these involved homosexual behaviour in public places. The term 'cottaging' is a British slang word used to describe the behaviour of gay men who 'hang around' outside public toilets waiting for sexual encounters. The term 'tea-housing' is the American equivalent. These terms are used as a form of irony, highlighting the contrast between public toilets and cosy comfortable places (Mills, 1993). One of the more high profile cases involved the pop singer George Michael, who was charged with 'lewd conduct' in a gents toilet in Los Angeles.

Female homosexuality and the law

Lesbian sex has never been illegal in Britain. It came very close in 1921, after the House of Commons passed a bill which criminalized it. However, it was

Table 3.5: *Cultural differences in attitudes and laws towards homosexuality*

Country	Legal status	Attitudes
India	Illegal	Anal intercourse with man, woman or animal 'goes against the order of nature'. Maximum sentence is life imprisonment
Malaysia	Illegal	Anal intercourse with man, woman or animal 'goes against the order of nature'. Maximum sentence is 20 years' imprisonment
Pakistan	Illegal	Anal intercourse with a man is viewed as 'going against the order of nature'. The penalty is between two years' and life imprisonment. Homosexuals are often viewed as social outcasts
Iran	Illegal	Homosexuality is viewed as 'one of the worst possible sins'. It is severely punished with whipping, stoning and even sentences of death
UK	Not illegal	The Sexual Offences Act 1967 decriminalized 'gay sex' in England and Wales. It was decriminalized in Scotland in 1981, and Northern Ireland in 1982.
Netherlands	Not illegal	

rejected by the House of Lords on the grounds that it might raise the profile of lesbianism, and entice women to try it, who had not previously heard of it.

Homosexuality and present-day cultural attitudes

As might be expected, homosexuality is viewed differently in different parts of the world. Table 3.5 identifies a number of countries and their laws regarding 'gay sex'.

Even within tribal cultures homosexual acceptance is found; some groups actively encourage it. In the Marind Anim society of New Guinea, semen is thought to promote growth and health. So ritualistic homosexual acts ensure young males receive it (Van Baal, 1966).

Female homosexuality (lesbianism)

As we have already seen, social attitudes towards lesbianism have always been more tolerant. This is true within most cultures. Within Westernized societies lesbianism is more covert. However, within some cultures, e.g. the Chukchee of Siberia and the Nama tribes of Africa, it is clearly overt.

In Victorian times lesbians were frequently referred to as 'romantic friends'. Even though lesbianism was tolerated far more than male homosexuality it was still perceived to be 'morally wrong' and perverted. The female parallel to Oscar Wilde was the author Radclyffe Hall. Her novel *The well of loneliness* (1928), which looked at lesbian relationships, was ordered to be destroyed by a London Court. In more recent times the term 'lesbianism' has been introduced. In many ways this creates a separate identity for female homosexuals, and is considered to be more 'politically correct'. The term derives from the Greek island 'Lesbos' which was home to Sappho (600 BC), the Greek poet who wrote about the beauty of the love between women.

Homosexuality as an illness

Until 1973, the American mental illness classification publication (DSM) had regarded homosexuality as a sexual deviation. Following a vote of a special committee of the American Psychiatric Association (1973), it was agreed that this term should be replaced with 'sexual orientation disturbance' (or to use medical jargon 'ego-dystonic homosexuality'). In reality this meant that if a man or woman was disturbed or unhappy with his or her homosexual orientation, clinicians would attempt to treat it. By the time the revised edition of DSM came out in 1989 (DSM-IIIR), views regarding homo-

sexuality had changed and no specific mention of homosexuality per se was used. The implication was that an individual could be unhappy with either sexual orientation, heterosexual and homosexual. Clearly, wider social changes towards homosexuality had influenced the medical profession. However, even today there is still a significant number of researchers who believe homosexuality is biological in origin and therefore potentially abnormal.

Explanations of homosexuality

Over the years various explanations have been put forward in an attempt to identify the underlying reasons as to why some people engage in homosexual behaviour. Before we look at some explanations it is important to stress that there are a number of broader underlying issues to consider.

By attempting to explain a behaviour we are forced to make a value judgement. How far we take that judgement is dependent upon many things including the 'norms' of a society and the influence of the media. For example, Wellings et al (1994) found that 70 per cent of British men believed that homosexuality is always or mostly wrong. Kinzinger and Coyle (1995) summarize Western perceptions when they state:

'Lesbian and gay couples are struggling to build and to maintain relationships in the context of a society which often denies their existence, condemns their sexuality, penalises their partnership and derides their love for each other.'

Any researcher working within a society will be influenced by his or her morality and beliefs. How often have you seen researchers attempt to explain why some people use credit cards or have ginger hair? There is no doubt homosexual behaviour appears to be a far more intriguing question.

By looking for an explanation we are attempting to isolate a reason (or reasons) for that behaviour existing. Heterosexuality has always been explainable through its links with reproduction. Because explanations of homosexuality are more complex, some researchers have taken this to reinforce its 'abnormality'.

If we find an explanation for a particular behaviour and in turn it is perceived to be abnormal, the next stage is to look for a cure. Prior to 1973, that is exactly what happened for many homosexual men. Drugs, penile electrodes and a multitude of psychotherapies were tried in order to 'cure' these men of their 'illness'. No 'cure' was ever found (Haldeman, 1994).

So the quest for explanations can in itself create stigmatization and prejudice. We will divide the explanations up into two groups: biological and psychosocial. Let us start with the biological ones.

Genetic explanations

One of the major problems with genetic explanations of any behaviour is that individuals with the same genotype (genetic makeup) may not present with the same phenotype (outward characteristics). Cultural, social, environmental and even hormonal fluctuations in the womb (*in utero*) can have a major influence on an individual's development both physically and behaviourally. Byrne (1994) summarizes the caution that should be exercised when he states that genes themselves specify proteins, not behavioural or psychological phenomena. Nevertheless, research into finding a 'gay gene' continues. One of the classic pieces of research into this was published by Hamer *et al*, in the journal *Science* (1993) (see RLA 12).

Real Life Application 12:

'The gay gene'

Early studies (e.g. those of Professor Richard Pillard, a Boston psychiatrist) found that the brother of a gay man had a fourfold increased chance of also being gay. This led scientists to question whether genetic influences were the source or whether it was a matter of environment (the brothers had been brought up in the same household). In 1992 Hamer *et al* found that there was an increased likelihood of homosexuality being passed from the maternal branches of the family tree. This was a intriguing finding because it suggested that 'being gay' was passed by the mother to her son. Males always receive their 'X' chromosome from their mother. Three years later Angela Pattatucci (1995) discovered that lesbians clustered in families. For example, a sister of a lesbian had a six times increased chance that she would be a lesbian also. What was quite amazing was that lesbian mothers had a one in three chance that their daughters would be 'gay' also.

In 1993, Hamer *et al* published a paper in the journal *Science*, which suggested there was a link between DNA markers on the X chromosome and male sexual orientation. Through analysing 40 pairs of gay brothers they had found a 'linkage' in a region called Xq28. Thirty-three out of 40 pairs of genes within this region seemed to be the same, indicating this group determined sexual orientation. Hamer goes on to speculate as to why a 'gay gene' still exists. He says:

'... how can a gene that leads to sexual behaviour that is nonreproductive survive the rough-and-tumble of evolution?'

This is a question which still has no satisfactory answer.

Adapted from 'Living with our genes'
by Hamer and Copeland, Pan, 1999

Summary

- Many early observations (including the work of Pillard) suggested that homosexuality ran in families.
- Research by Hamer and Pattatucci showed that there appeared to be 'genes' responsible for homosexuality.
- In 1993 Hamer *et al* identified a region of the X chromosome in men (Xq28), which they believe is responsible for sexual orientation.

Questions

1 In your own words summarize the research into a 'gay gene'.

2 What are the 'pros and cons' of suggesting that sexual orientation is determined by our genes?

Hormonal explanations

One of the earliest hormonal explanations was proposed by Feldman and MacCollough in 1971. They argued that homosexual males escaped the correct exposure to circulating male hormones while *in utero* leading to their bodies being masculinized (correct male sexual organs) but making their sexual preferences female. Less commonly, female foetuses accidentally become exposed to a high level of male hormones *in utero* making their sexual preferences male.

Commentary

In order to understand this hormonal explanation more fully, it must be pointed out that all embryos start off 'female'. In development nature has made the female body the 'norm'. Because a male embryo carries a Y chromosome, this kick-starts a process by which males produce more male hormones, thereby masculinizing the developing foetus into a sexually competent male. Clearly, this is a more complex process than producing females, therefore potentially there is more chance of something going wrong. Some commentators believe this could explain the higher incidence of male homosexuality than lesbianism (Stevens and Price, 1996). Despite these interesting ideas, the pre-natal hormonal explanation still requires more research.

Evolutionary explanations

As we saw in RLA 12, scientists have been 'hard pushed' to explain the evolutionary benefits of homosexuality. Sex which precludes reproduction must have some evolutionary benefit, otherwise it would have disappeared from the human genome. What could the benefits be? In order to find an answer 'evolutionists' turned their attention to the animal kingdom.

Homosexual behaviour in the animal kingdom

Homosexual behaviour is seen in many species of animal, from the parasitic worm to the 'Bluegill Sunfish' (Sommer, 1990). However many researchers have turned their attention to our primate relatives. Because primates are social animals and have such well-defined social hierarchies, they are ideal when studying a behaviour which has both biological and social dimensions.

Mutual masturbation has been observed by some stump-tailed macaques and some rhesus monkeys have even shown a preference for homosexual relationships over heterosexual; however, this is rare in the animal kingdom in general (Werner, 1995). Most homosexual behaviour within primates has been interpreted as a way of maintaining the status quo. Social rank is everything in monkey troops and expressions of dominance and subordination are often sexual in nature. In groups of rhesus monkeys for example, it is only 20 per cent of the males who perform 80 per cent of the copulations. The males are always the most dominant. Fifty per cent never copulate at all (Stevens and Price, 1996). Wilson (1989) argues this primate strategy makes evolutionary sense. If the dominant 'stronger' males provide the majority of the reproduction, then it will be their genes that are passed from one generation to the next.

Relating animal studies to humans

On the face of it, primate studies of homosexuality seem to suggest that homosexuals must be inferior and subordinate. In evolutionary theory this is known as the dominance failure theory. Another explanation suggests that just as in primate troops, homosexual males do not produce any offspring themselves, thereby keeping the population down. This would mean the 'dominant homosexual gene' does not get passed on, however the homosexuals could help their relatives raise more offspring (this is known as the kin selection hypothesis). Thirdly, the other major evolutionary explanation is that the 'recessive homosexual gene' (that is one which is carried by an individual but doesn't present) could have some reproductive advantage (as yet unknown) when combined with heterosexual genes (this is known as the heterozygous hypothesis).

Let us now look at some psychosocial explanations.

Early childhood experiences

As part of Freud's psychosexual theory of development, he proposed that homosexuality was primarily a 'fixation' which occurred during the phallic stage (Freud, 1910). Freud talks specifically about the 'oedipal' conflict, in which the young boy becomes fearful of competing with his father for his mother's affections. This fear according to Freud generalizes to all women. In an attempt to deal with this inner psychic turmoil the boy identifies with his mother rather than his father (the normal path of development according to Freud). It is this identification to the female role model which ultimately leads to a homosexual orientation. So according to psychoanalytical theory homosexuality is created early in childhood, but does not manifest until adolescence.

Commentary

There is very little evidence to substantiate Freudian theory. Surveys looking into the childhood of homosexuals have found very little difference between their early childhood experiences and that of a heterosexual control group (Bell *et al*, 1981). Bieber (1976) did find, however, that homosexual males had disturbed relationships with their fathers. They were described as 'detached' or openly hostile, so the young male grew up 'craving' the love and affection of his father.

Childhood experiences and lesbianism

Charlotte Wolf (1971) carried out a similar programme of research prior to Bieber's work, looking at childhood experiences of lesbians. She found that homosexual women tended to have a rejecting or indifferent mother, and a distant or absent father. Wolf argued that young girls spend the rest of their life seeking the love and affection of women (as a substitute for their earlier insufficiency) and because of a distant father are never able to relate to men.

Social learning theories

Social learning theory assumes that humans (like many other animal species) are 'generally unspecific' in their sexual orientation. It is environmental or social rewards or punishments that determine which direction their sexual preferences will be directed. In simple terms people are born sexual. Which direction their sexuality takes will be determined by social experiences.

Commentary

There are two pieces of evidence that make social learning theory difficult to accept. Firstly, in Western society heterosexuality is overwhelmingly positively endorsed. There are few rewards for being homosexual. So why is anyone homosexual (Whitam, 1977)? Secondly, studies have shown that the majority of children who grow up with homosexual parents are unlikely to become homosexual themselves (Green, 1978). Clearly, they do not learn from their parents.

Homosexuality in Melanesia

One final piece of evidence that suggests homosexuality is constructed and defined by society (therefore psychosocial) comes from cross-cultural research in Melanesia, an area of the south-west Pacific. Great significance is placed upon 'ritualistic homosexual acts' between an adult male and an adolescent boy. It is viewed as a 'rite of passage' for the young male into adulthood. Also it is believed that 'semen' aids growth in puberty. In all cases the young man is expected to grow up heterosexual, marry and have children (Schieffelin, 1976).

Commentary

Findings such as these illustrate two important points. Firstly, sexual orientation is more than just biology. Cultural norms define what is acceptable and what is not. The same behaviour in Britain is illegal, and the adult responsible would go to prison. Secondly, it illustrates that an individual's 'sexual identity' and his or her 'sexual behaviour' can be different. Adult Melanesian males

would not define themselves as gay, even though they had all engaged in homosexual behaviours.

Homosexuality and the nature–nurture debate

So what is the answer to the origins of homosexuality? Within psychology as a whole, an age-old question continually resurfaces. It is referred to as the nature–nurture debate and it focuses on the question of whether behaviour is genetic (nature) or learnt (nurture). Table 3.6 summarizes the key studies that have been considered, and places them on the relevant side of the debate.

Table 3.6: Studies which give weight to the nature–nurture debate regarding homosexuality

Nature (biological)	Nurture (psychosocial)
Genetics: Hamer *et al*, 1993	*Unconscious conflicts:* Freud, 1910
Hormones: Feldman and MacCollough, 1971; Stevens and Price (1996)	*Parental influence:* Bieber, 1976; Wolf, 1971
Evolutionary: Sommer, 1990; Werner, 1995; Wilson, 1989	*Cross-cultural:* Schieffelin, 1976

Clearly, no one factor emerges as the 'cause' of homosexuality and lesbianism. Part of the problem could be that most research assumes that homosexuals are all the same. They form a homogeneous group. Bell and Weinberg (1978) argued that it would be more useful to use the term 'homosexualities' acknowledging the fact that all 'gays' are different. Having now looked at different preferences regarding sexual behaviour, we will finally look at the risks involved in engaging in 'intimate sexual relationships'.

The risks of sexual relationships

As we have already seen, engaging in sexual behaviour fulfils a fundamental need in humans, by allowing them to be intimate with another person. However, there have always been 'risks'. The following list identifies some examples.

Emotional risks

- Engaging in a sexual relationship without having sufficient 'depth of feelings' for the other person. This is likely to lead to the other person feeling rejected and the instigator feeling guilty.
- Wanting to engage in a sexual relationship but being rejected. This leaves the individual feeling hurt and humiliated.

- Being publicly humiliated for engaging in a sexual liaison. (The relationship between US President Bill Clinton and Monica Lewinsky is a good example.) This can lead to feelings of anger, guilt and humiliation. What is usually an intimate, private behaviour has become public.

Physical risks

- Engaging in 'unprotected' casual sex with a stranger. This can increase the chances of contracting a sexually transmitted disease (STD).
- Having a casual sexual liaison while already in a stable sexual relationship. This increases the chances of the stable partner contracting a STD.

The following are examples of STDs:

- **Gonorrhea** – this is possibly the oldest of all STDs. References were made to it in the Bible (Leviticus 15). Hippocrates (400 BC) proposed it was caused by 'excessive indulgences in the pleasures of Venus' (hence venereal disease). Neisser identified the bacterium that caused it in 1879. One problem with this disease is that it does not always present symptoms (asymptomatic). This increases the chances of infection through casual sexual liaisons. The person looks fine. It is treatable with high doses of penicillin.
- **Chlamydia** – this is a STD more commonly found in higher socio-economic groups, particularly university students. It can be treated with tetracycline or erythromycin.
- **Genital herpes** – this disease is caused by the 'Herpes simplex' virus. Unfortunately, once an individual has the disease they have it for life, with 'flare-ups' occurring every so often. Increasing sexual partners increases the risk of infection.
- **Syphilis** – no one is quite sure of the origins of syphilis. One theory suggests it was introduced to Europe by Columbus after his first voyage to the West Indies in 1493. In 1905 two German scientists Shauddin and Hoffman identified the bacterium which causes it. If left untreated it can lead to serious conditions and in extreme cases can be fatal. It is treatable with long-acting penicillin.

All these diseases are spread through sexual behaviour and can be very unpleasant. However, no one could have been prepared for a disease which started to emerge in the early 1980s.

HIV and AIDS

In 1981 a physician working in Los Angeles reported a mysterious disease which he identified in several gay men. Within two years the number of victims had escalated and the world was introduced to Acquired Immune Deficiency Syndrome (AIDS). In 1984 Gallo identified the virus causing AIDS. It was initially called HTLV-3, but now it is called HIV (Human Immunodeficiency Virus).

Incidence of the disease

It was estimated by the United Nations Joint Nations Programme on HIV/AIDS (UNAIDS) in a worldwide survey in 1996 that there were 22.6 million people infected with HIV/AIDS, 90 per cent of whom live in the developing world. Worst affected regions were Sub-Saharan Africa (with an estimated 14 million sufferers) and South/South-East Asia with an estimated 5.2 million. Least affected areas were Australasia (with an estimated 13,000 sufferers) and eastern Europe and Central Asia (with an estimated 50,000 sufferers).

More than 90 per cent of cases in the USA have been men, so many still view it as a 'gay disease'. However, AIDS in Africa affects men and women in roughly equal numbers. It has been suggested that globally, over 70 per cent of all HIV infections are contracted through heterosexual intercourse (cited by Fullick, 1998). Drug misuse is the second most common cause of infection. In a study conducted in the USA, Guinan and Hardy (1987) found that more than 50 per cent of women who had AIDS, had contracted it through intravenous drug use.

Changing individuals' behaviour

Clearly, the most obvious way to prevent AIDs (including other STDs as well) is to develop ways of 'changing risky sexual behaviours'. This would allow people to still be intimate, but significantly reduce their risk of contracting diseases. During the 1980s there were many advertising campaigns launched across the world to do just this. Probably, one of the most memorable ones in Britain was of a picture of a gravestone with the inscription 'AIDS – don't die of ignorance'.

However, research showed that these campaigns were not as successful as had been hoped. A survey, conducted by the Wellcome Trust on 'sexual attitudes and lifestyles' in 1994, found that although the message (of using condoms) appeared to be getting through, there was little evidence that other forms of 'safe sex practices' were being adopted. In fact, suggestions of reducing the numbers of sexual partners, or restricting 'casual sex' liaisons appeared to be ignored. Changing attitudes of something as personal as 'intimate behaviour' appears to be present enormous challenges.

Commentary

There has been considerable effort spent assessing the reasons why individuals are reluctant to change their behaviours in the face of a potentially lethal disease. Possibly the two most frequently cited suggestions centre around people's perceptions of risk. Weinstein (1987) developed the concept of 'unrealistic optimism'. He argued that people believe themselves to be invulnerable, therefore cannot see the point of changing their behaviours, however potentially risky. White *et al* (1989) found that university students tended to favour 'vetting' the past sexual histories of potential partners as the most popular method of reducing risk. Clearly, for well-informed and educated individuals, this was highly

unreliable. It does, however, confirm something we have consistently found throughout this chapter. When it comes to our most intimate relationships, logic appears to 'go out the window'.

Essay questions

1 Outline and evaluate the ways in which psychologists have attempted to explain love.

2 In what ways does cross-cultural research suggest that marriage is a 'socially defined' concept?

3 Homosexual relationships are fundamentally different from heterosexual. Discuss.

Contemporary issues

This chapter is divided into two sections. Section 1 begins by looking at issues regarding the family. It considers alternative lifestyles such as co-habitation, communes and solitary lifestyles including hermits. It also looks at the issues of gay couples adopting children. Next it focuses on domestic violence and rape. Thirdly, it assesses the impact of stessors upon the family. In particular, it looks at the effects of a newborn baby, illness, disability and bereavement. Finally, it looks at couples and family therapy. Real Life Applications that are considered are:

- RLA 13: Gay couples and adoption
- RLA 14: Domestic violence
- RLA 15: Smacking children
- RLA 16: Rohypnol – the date rape drug
- RLA 17: Rape makes evolutionary sense!
- RLA 18: Relate – the couples counselling agency.

Section 2 considers three further contemporary issues. It starts by looking at loneliness and the effects of urbanization on communities. It then considers electronic media and their effects on relationships. Finally, human relationships with animals and pets are discussed. Real Life Applications considered are:

- RLA 19: Neighbourhood loneliness
- RLA 20: A virtual neighbourhood
- RLA 21: Walking the dog – 'a good social exercise'.

SECTION 1

Marriage and alternative lifestyles

We have already looked at marriage as an 'institution' in Chapter 3. In this section we are going to consider a few alternatives to marriage. We will start by considering cohabitation, then we will look at communes. Next, hermits and people in isolated religious groups will be considered. Finally, the issues regarding gay couples adopting children will be explored.

Cohabitation

Over the past ten years or so, there has been a decline in the number of people living as married couples; however there has been an increase in couples **cohabiting** (living together in the same property as an unmarried couple). The proportion of all non-married women aged 18–49 who were cohabiting in the UK has doubled since 1981, to 25 per cent in 1996–7 (*Social Trends,* 1999). Figure 4.1 shows that women aged 24–34 are the most likely age group to cohabit. Incidentally, this is the most likely age range in men as well; however women outnumbered men (in 1996–7) in the actual proportion of cohabitations (19 per cent of men, 31 per cent of women).

Commentary

There are many explanations given in an attempt to explain the increase in cohabitation. Many couples when interviewed stress the benefits of 'relationship flexibility'. Couples are not 'tying' themselves to a legal contract. It gives them an opportunity to give their relationship a 'probationary period'. Politically right-wing commentators have argued cohabitation is a sign of the breakdown of the family – 'an undermining of traditional family values'. Fletcher (1988) points out that perhaps cohabitation is not as extreme as some would have us believe. Even though couples live together and have

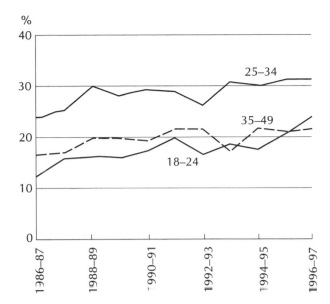

Figure 4.1: Percentage of women cohabiting by age, Britain, 1986–97, (Source: 'Social trends,' Office for National Statistics © Crown Copyright 2000)

children without legitimizing their relationship by law, they are still conforming to a model of a stable traditional nuclear family.

Communes

The *Oxford English Dictionary* defines a commune as:

'a group of people, not all of one family, sharing accommodation and goods'.

Over the years, 'commune style' living has fluctuated in terms of its popularity. The establishment of 'hippie colonies' during the 1960s heralded a major revival in alternative lifestyles, offering young people a chance to 'drop out' of conventional society. History is littered with examples of small groups of people escaping from the society of their time, and attempting to set up 'Utopian communities'.

The Oneida commune

A classic example of this was an American colony started in the 1830s by John Humphrey Noyes. His desire was to create a Christian communist Utopia (Van den Berghe, 1979), based in Oneida, New York. During their peak they boasted over 500 men, women and children. They farmed communal land and manufactured steel products which were sold to the outside world. Each adult had his or her own room, but everything else was shared including clothes, childcare and even sex partners. Noyes ruled that romantic love between particular couples

was selfish, and therefore forbidden. Everyone was expected to copulate with everyone else. Despite Noyes' ruling, couples did form and in 1879 the commune was disbanded.

Commentary

The idea that humans are best suited to more intimate groupings rather than commune living, was summarized by Margaret Mead when she said:

'No matter how many communes anybody invents, the family always creeps back' (Mead, 1935).

A kibbutz

Another good example of a commune is the Israeli kibbutz. Couples usually form pairs and marry, however their children are viewed as the responsibility of the commune as a whole. Certain members of the group are specially trained to bring up children (known as the metapalet – or care-giver) The children live in a separate 'children's house' and visit their parents each day.

Commentary

Does this experience affect a child's attachment and bonding behaviour?

Some of the early work suggested no. Fox (1977) showed that 'secure attachment' behaviours existed for both the biological mother and the metapalet. However, more recent work (e.g. Sagi *et al*, 1985) identified more ambivalent attachment behaviours of children raised on a kibbutz, when compared with their American and Israeli 'family-raised' counterparts. So the evidence appears to be mixed.

Does this experience affect a child's pro-social development?

Studies have shown that children raised on a kibbutz show a higher level of community awareness, when presented with moral dilemmas (Eisenberg *et al*, 1990). It appears contributing to the needs of the community is of paramount importance. Studies have also shown that kibbutz-raised children are able to demonstrate higher levels of co-operation during play than children from Westernized cultures (Shapira and Madsen, 1969).

The above evidence suggests that the ethos of the culture in which children are raised, has a major effect on their behaviour. Communes stress co-operation, and loss of individualism.

Hermits and isolated religious groups

We have just considered the lifestyles of people who live in communes and found that an overriding feature is co-operation and interdependence. As we saw in Chapter 1, evolutionary theories suggest these behaviours were exhibited by our ancient ancestors, providing nurturance and protection. But what of people who 'drop out of society' not to join a chosen community, but to lead a life of solitude?

Hermits

The *Oxford English Dictionary* defines a hermit as:

'a person (especially a man in early Christian times) who has withdrawn from human society and lives in solitude'.

One important distinction to make is that choice plays a vital role in understanding the life of a hermit. Solitude is different to loneliness, in so much as the former has been an individual's choice, whereas the latter has not. Hermits choose a solitary lifestyle.

Isolated religious groups

Throughout history, groups of men and women have withdrawn from society and adopted a life of isolation, contemplation and prayer. Even today groups exist where contact with the outside world is highly limited.

Spiritual leaders such as Jesus Christ, Gandhi and Martin Luther King went through important periods of prolonged solitude. During these times they discovered more completely their own sense of mission. But what underlying psychology can motivate and encourage a person to live a life of minimal social contact? Researchers such as Kirkpatrick (1994) suggest that many religions (but primarily Christian), perceive a personal relationship with God. This develops in the same way as 'human relationships', with strength of 'emotional attachment' being a primary indicator of how successful the relationship is. In a strong relationship with God a person can:

- maintain regular contact through prayer (proximity seeking)
- find security and reassurance (the 'secure base')
- find comfort and support in times of distress (a 'safe haven').

Commentary

Kirkpatrick's ideas give an interesting explanation as to how religious hermits can maintain a life of solitude. It is not their religious beliefs that help sustain their isolation, but their levels of attachment to God. It is not so much a cognitive process as an emotional one. Indeed,

Kirkpatrick and Shaver (1992) demonstrated that cognitive measures of religiosity are not related to psychological well-being, whereas measures of secure attachment to God are.

It appears, living a life of religious solitude is good for your mind as well as your soul.

The alternative family unit – gay couples adopting

The idea of homosexuals adopting and raising children continues to be a highly contentious issue. In 1997 the *Guardian* reported the case of Russell Conlon and his partner Chris Joyce (both homosexuals) and their battle to adopt a child.

'We are prepared to do anything for a child,' Mr Conlon said. *'We feel that the love and respect which a child brings would complete our lives.'*

He went on to say:

'I know that we would be brilliant parents. We love each other very much and in the eyes of God we are married.'

Chris Joyce said:

'I have wanted children all my life and now I've found the right person.'

More recently, Tony Barlow and Barrie Drewitt became the first gay couple to father surrogate twins (see RLA 13 on p. 77).

A number of issues arise when considering the debate regarding homosexual adoption. We will look at them in turn and review the evidence.

1 The children of homosexual parents will grow up to be homosexual

This is probably the most common argument given regarding adoption. However, several studies have shown that children adopted by homosexual parents are no more or less likely to show homosexual behaviour in later life than children raised by heterosexual parents (Bailey *et al*, 1995; Tasker and Golombok, 1995).

2 It is 'unnatural' for a child to live in a 'gay family'

Many moral commentators argue the 'unnaturalness' of the 'gay family'. Many of their assertions are based upon evolutionary ideas of procreation or religious ideologies. The Revd Ian Brown, vicar of Halliwell, near Bolton, was quoted as saying:

'This is the wrong environment in which to bring up chil-

dren. It must be very confusing to have two mums and two dads' (Brown, 1997).

Baroness Warnock, a moral philosopher, commented:

'I suspect if you decide to live with a homosexual partner you've got to forgo bringing up a child. It's not a right' (Warnock, 1997).

3 Children within homosexual families will be abused

Unlike heterosexuality, homosexuality still suffers the legacy of once being classed as a mental disorder. In a recent survey 70 per cent of men thought homosexual behaviour was always or mostly wrong (British Sexual Attitudes Survey, 1994). The argument is that this potentially abnormal lifestyle could put children in danger of being abused. However, homosexual activists argue that this is a myth.

'A far smaller proportion of abuse goes on in lesbian and gay households. Abuse is about power' (Bellos, 1997).

4 Homosexual relationships are not stable for children

There is some evidence that homosexuals are highly promiscuous (particularly males). Bell and Weinberg (1978) reported the following statistics regarding promiscuity:

- 74 per cent of male homosexuals reported having more than 100 sexual partners in their lifetime
- 28 per cent of male homosexuals reported having more than a 1000 partners
- 10 per cent of male homosexuals claimed to be in a steady relationship
- 28 per cent of lesbians claimed to be in a steady relationship.

As with abuse, the question of parental stability is not based upon sexual orientation but the individual parents themselves. Many children within heterosexual families are exposed to abuse and promiscuity.

5 Is it illegal in Britain for 'gays and lesbians' to adopt?

In British law there is nothing to stop a gay man or woman individually adopting a child, subject to approval. In reality this is rare. Some research carried out at Cardiff University in 1998 found that only three out of 2000 approved adoptions were by gays.

6 Is there is a need to include 'lesbian and gay' couples in adoption?

Because of the arguments against homosexual adoption some people would argue that there is no need to include lesbian and gay couples in adoption. However, Felicity Collier, chief executive of the British Agencies for Adoption and Fostering, points out that there are not enough people coming forward for fostering (Collier, 2000).

Real Life Application 13: Gay couples and adoption

Material A – A moral issue?

Evidence for:
One issue which continues to create controversy is whether gay couples should be able to adopt children. The Prime Minister, Tony Blair, is proposing a new national adoption scheme which will force councils to consider gay and unmarried couples' applications, which most reject at present. He believes many homosexuals in stable relationships are being unfairly denied the chance to adopt.

Evidence against:
At present nearly 1300 would-be parents are waiting to adopt. In British law there is nothing to stop gay couples adopting, subject to approval by the adoption agency. However, in reality, few applications are granted. Research at Cardiff University in 1998 found that three out of 2000 approved adoptions were by gays. Valerie Riches, director of Family and Youth Concern, said:

'This government is beholden to the gay lobby. It is very serious for the institution of marriage, which is the safest and best way to bring up children.'

Rosemary Keenan of Westminster Catholic Children's Society said:

'There is no formal recognition of gay marriage and it's inappropriate morally for children to be brought up outside marriage.'

Material B – gay surrogate fathers: a case study

A gay couple who fathered surrogate twins are set to have a third child. Millionaire businessmen Tony Barlow and Barrie Drewitt said:

'We are determined to go for three children.'

Tony Barlow and Barry Drewitt with their surrogate twins

The pair are no strangers to controversy. They were the first gay couple to father surrogate twins when they paid an American woman £200,000 to have Aspen and Saffron.

A spokesman for the Family Welfare Association said:

'Traditional family values seem to have gone out of the window. No one seems to have taken the children into account here.'

Dr Adrian Rogers, adviser to Family Focus, a pro-family campaign, said:

'To deprive the child of one of its natural sexual role models should be a crime.'

Article adapted from 'Gay dads' baby No. 3' by John Troup and Paul Thompson, *The Sun*, 1 June 2000.

Summary

- The Labour government, in June 2000, was considering 'forcing' councils to treat gay and unmarried couples in the same way when assessing them for suitability to adopt.
- Research at Cardiff University (1998) found three out of 2000 approved adoptions were by gay couples.
- Many 'pro-traditional family' groups see gays adopting children as a breakdown in 'traditional family values'.

Questions

1 What is meant by 'traditional family values'?

2 Discuss the psychological evidence 'for' and 'against' homosexuals adopting children.

Domestic violence

A perception of the family being a 'haven' of safety and security is an image all of us like to hold. As we have already seen in Chapter 1, the notion of a 'secure base' is vital for emotional stability. A 'home' as opposed to a house (a description of the building itself) can act for many as their 'secure base'. Sadly, for many this image is not the case. It is very difficult to estimate the extent of domestic violence, because by its very nature it occurs behind closed doors, however it does appear to be on the increase (see RLA 14). Just to emphasize the point that families are not always the safe places we want them to be, statistics show that one in four murders in the UK is committed by one family member against another (cited in Giddens, 1997).

Real Life Application 14: Domestic violence

An epidemic of domestic violence is sweeping Britain's homes. Research carried out by the Racial and Violent Task Force, has revealed that out of 8000 incidents that they deal with each month, 76 per cent are domestic, 22 per cent are racial and 2 per cent are targeted at homosexuals (homophobic). In the West Midlands (see Figure 4.2) where the crime rate has remained relatively stable for the past four years, domestic violence has risen from 14,011 (1996–7) to 25,225 (1999–2000).

Social scientists and women's groups are working together in an attempt to explain the increase. The government blames changes in society as a whole. The Metropolitan Police have recently extended their definition of domestic violence to include threatening behaviour. This can include threatened physical violence,

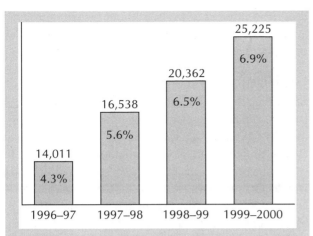

Figure 4.2: Incidents of domestic violence (percentage of domestic violence against total crime)

psychological, sexual, financial or emotional threats, between adults who are or were partners or family. In practice these definitions will be very hard to implement.

Domestic violence – the statistics

- There are 250 refuge groups in England. Of 54,500 annual admissions to refuges, 32,000 are children.
- Four-fifths of domestic violence on women involves partners or ex-partners.
- Every year one in ten women in Britain experiences domestic violence.

  Adapted from article by Martin Bright, *The Observer*, 16 July 2000.

Summary

- Statistics show that there is an increase in reported domestic violence.
- In the West Midlands domestic crime rates have risen from 14,011 incidents to 25,225.
- The Metropolitan Police have increased the number of behaviours they class as domestic violence.

Questions

1 Give two possible reasons why domestic violence has increased.

2 Based upon your psychological knowledge, what ways are there of reducing domestic violence?

Who are the victims?

Studies have shown that the prime targets of physical abuse are children (see p. 81). Violence by males against women (usually husbands against wives) are the second most frequent target (see p. 80), and lastly women against their children or husbands (see p. 82). A study conducted by Mooney (1993) looked at types of violence women had experienced over their lifetimes. Table 4.1 gives some examples from this work. Table 4.2 shows who the women turned to for help.

Table 4.1: The frequency (percentage) of different types of violence women have experienced, based upon Mooney (1993)

Violent behaviours	Percentage
Mental cruelty	37
Including verbal abuse (e.g. the calling of names, being ridiculed in front of other people)	
Threats of violence or force	27
Actual physical violence	
Grabbed or pushed or shaken	32
Punched or slapped	25
Kicked	14
Head butted	6
Attempted strangulation	9
Hit with a weapon/object	8
Injuries	
Injured	27
Bruising or black eye	26
Scratches	12
Cuts	11
Bones broken	6
Rape (made to have sex without consent)	23
Rape with threats of violence	13
Rape with physical violence	9

Table 4.1 indicates that mental violence represented the highest percentage. Table 4.2 shows that most of the women who had been victims turned to friends as their primary source of confiding.

Women are usually reluctant to report their husband's/partner's crime for many reasons. They include:

- fear of further violence
- self blame (they see themselves as deserving what they got)
- being embarrassed (perhaps because they feel people may ask questions such as 'Why did you marry him in the first place?')
- a belief that the police are not interested

Table 4.2: The frequency (percentage) of different sources of help used by women, based upon Mooney (1993)

Of those experiencing violence the following people and agencies were informed	Violence at any time (%)	Violence in last 12 months (%)
Friend	46	36
Relative	31	29
General practitioner	22	17
Police	22	14
Solicitor	21	12
Social Services	9	7
Women's refuge	5	3
Victim support	2	1
Citizen's Advice Bureau	2	1

Commentary

In the 1970s women's refuges were set up, funded by local councils, for female victims to go to escape from violent homes. Most large cities have them today. Also in 1996, the Family Homes and Domestic Violence Bill made provision for violent individuals to be excluded from family homes. However, neither of these addresses the problem of why domestic violence occurs in the first place.

Explanations for domestic violence

Research has shown that domestic violence occurs for many reasons, therefore finding simple solutions is extremely difficult. A selection of explanations is outlined below.

Biological explanations

In Chapter 1 we looked at evolutionary and biological explanations of relationship behaviour. The role of hormones was discussed, and in particular the role of testosterone in male sexual behaviour. For many years, studies have linked this hormone to aggressive behaviour, particularly in animals (see Chapter 1, p. 12). Darwin (1871) suggested that men were more aggressive, on average, and women do more nurturing. A number of studies have shown that aggression is associated with sex differences, even in childhood. Macoby and Jacklin (1974) have shown that boys tend to be more physically aggressive than girls. However, these ideas do not explain why domestic violence occurs, they only suggest that males are more likely to be the perpetrators of it.

Genetic links?

A study conducted by Stevenson (1999) suggested that people who are bullies, produce offspring who are also bullies. A conclusion from the study was that the tendency to bully is about 60 per cent controlled by genes and 40 per cent controlled by upbringing and environment.

Commentary

According to researchers such as Leakey and Lewin (1977), cultural influences are far more important determinants of human aggressive behaviour than biological factors. Moore (1998) gives some possible reasons as to why men engage in more domestic violence than women. In summary he suggests that Western culture endorses a 'macho' image of men being tough. This can be seen portrayed through books, films and advertising. Violence against partners within this context is explained through 'role modelling'.

Indeed, Mead (1935) reported in her studies of different societies in New Guinea that culture shapes how men and women behave. In the Arapesh tribe, both men and women were brought up to be co-operative, gentle, caring and non-aggressive. Male acts of aggression towards women were unheard of. Clearly, in this culture, domestic violence was not an inevitability of male hormones. Even though Mead's observations are interesting, recent questions have been raised regarding the validity of her work (e.g. Freeman, 1983).

The need to control

One reason why some men engage in violent behaviour is in an attempt to assert their control over a dysfunctional relationship (Moore, 1998). This dysfunction can lead to feelings of frustration. Is it inevitable that frustration would lead to aggression? Berkowitz (1966) proposed that frustration leads to feelings of anger. It is the presence of a 'suitable environmental cue' which translates anger into violence and 'the partner' is perceived as a 'suitable target'.

Poor role models and anger management

Learning theory suggests that violence is a response acquired in childhood. Many children who are exposed to aggressive role models in childhood (particularly parents) are likely to resort to violence as a means of conflict management (Davison and Neale, 1998). Further evidence argues that men who find it difficult to communicate their feelings or to handle anger are more likely to engage in violent behaviour (Eckhardt et al, 1997).

Commentary

Apart from the ideas discussed above, many other factors have been linked to male domestic violence. Holtzworth-Munroe *et al* (1995) identify environmental factors such as stress, alcohol usage, drug abuse and social factors such as possessing a negative attitude towards women. However, it must be remembered all these factors may exacerbate a violent tendency but they do not cause it.

Child abuse

This term refers to sexual, physical or emotional mistreatment of minors. The Children Act 1989 defines the rights of children and the course of action should abuse be identified. A survey conducted by the National Children's Homes (1992) suggested that between 12 per cent and 59 per cent of all women and between 8 per cent and 27 per cent of all men have experienced some form of sexual abuse before the age of 18.

Who abuses and why?

Many commentators assume that the primary perpetrators of child sexual abuse are fathers, stepfathers, grandfathers or other males close to the child. However, statistics are notoriously unreliable in this area.

Smacking children – a form of child abuse?

Philip Hodson (1999), a fellow of the British Association for Counselling, wrote an article that highlighted the dangers of smacking children. He proposed that there is no need to smack children, and any act of violence (however minor) can potentially lead to more serious offences, possibly physical child abuse (see RLA 15).

Real Life Application 15:

Smacking children

Philip Hodson (1999) cites Paul Boateng's (a Parliamentary under-secretary to the Ministry of Health) assertion that:

'smacking has a place within parental discipline and our law will not be changed'.

He is concerned by stories of extreme violence towards children. Groups such as 'self-styled' parenting gurus, Gary and Anne-Marie Ezzo, claim to have 'educated' more than 1.5 million parents worldwide in how to bring up their children. Their message is simple: 'hitting 'em while they are still young' is the only way to instil a 'lifetime of obedience'.

Hodson goes on to suggest that people such as the Ezzos must be 'deluded' if they believe beating a child is 'an act of love'. He argues that we do not live in a society where parents are always right. There is evidence that spanking by parents leads to anti-social behaviour in children. He concludes by saying that Mr Boateng must 'come off the fence on this issue' and outlaw abusive parental behaviour.

Summary

- The government, in 1999, believed that 'smacking had a place within parental discipline'.
- Hodson, cites the ideas of so-called 'family gurus', such as Gary and Ann-Marie Ezzo, as an example of abuse masquerading as discipline.
- Hodson suggests the government should ban the smacking of children.

Questions

1 Why could smacking be seen as a form of physical child abuse?

2 What would be the difficulties and implications in introducing a ban on smacking?

Incest

Incest is a term used to refer to sexual relations between close relatives for whom marriage is forbidden. The current scientific view is that this taboo makes medical sense. There is an increased risk of inheriting birth defects if close relatives produce offspring. Therefore, there appears to be an adaptive evolutionary benefit in having an incest taboo (Geer *et al*, 1984).

There is evidence that families in which incest takes place are unusually patriarchal (e.g. Alexander and Lupfer, 1987). A high proportion of child abuse (up to half) is committed by adolescent males (Becker, 1995). Many of these come from homes that are dysfunctional (Blaske *et al*, 1989) and many were themselves abused as children (Worling, 1996). Compared to criminals who have been convicted of non-sexual offences, child abusers have been found to be more socially isolated and possess fewer social skills (Awad and Saunders, 1989).

Women who 'beat' their partners

As we have seen, statistically speaking it is less common for women physically to abuse their partners. It is often believed that because (on average) a woman is less physically strong than a man, physical assault will be less severe. Indeed, studies do suggest that 'husband beating' is much less likely to result in serious injury to the victim (e.g. Holtzworth-Munroe and Stuart, 1994). Of course, this assumes that the woman does not use an implement of some description to inflict her aggression.

Straus and Gelles (1986) proposed that on average, one American male is assaulted by his wife every 14 seconds. So why do the statistics imply that domestic violence only occurs to women and children? Certain factors could contribute to this distorted picture including the following:

- Men feel embarrassed to report domestic violence to third parties.
- There are no male refuges to escape to.
- Western culture maintains an ethos that men should be tough and physically resilient.

Commentary

Mead (1935) studied the Mundugamor tribe of New Guinea, and found that both sexes were equally aggressive. Indeed, females were encouraged to be aggressive and fight for what they wanted, even if that meant physically competing with males. So the Mundugamor would not perceive 'husband beating' as an issue – for them it was a cultural norm.

Women who kill their offspring

One major event which temporarily changes the balance of the hormonal system of a female is pregnancy and childbirth. Regardless of the type of pregnancy experienced, or the family situation, between 50 per cent and 80 per cent of all women develop the 'maternity blues' during the first week after childbirth. Interestingly, this appears to be a consistent finding in different cultures and ethnic groups, indicating a biological cause rather than a social one (referred to in Goldberg *et al*, 1994). For most mothers their symptoms of mood swings are brief. However, occasionally a more serious condition can develop known as post-natal depression. There is a small but definite risk that the mother will kill her child. If she kills her child within one year and one day, this is known as 'infanticide' and is dealt with in British law as manslaughter rather than murder. The *Oxford English Dictionary* defines infanticide as: *'murder of an infant soon after its birth'.*

Approximately half the women who commit infanticide also commit suicide (referred to in Goldberg *et al*, 1994).

Commentary

Most psychiatrists are in agreement that there are fundamental differences between the offenders of physical child abuse and infanticide. Females who abuse their offspring are not on the whole physiologically imbalanced unlike the perpetrators of infanticide. Like male abusers they tend to have poor communication skills and seek domination and power. However, socio-economic factors can also lead to infanticide in certain cultures. In China (where families are limited to having one child), over a quarter of a million girls were killed after their birth between 1979 and 1984 (Ridley, 1993). This horrendous statistic shows the importance Chinese families place on having their only child 'a male'.

Rape

Of all the types of violent crime rape is arguably the most repulsive. In legal terms there are two main categories of rape:

1 Forced rape – sexual intercourse with an unwilling partner.
2 Statutory rape – sexual intercourse between a male and female minor (under the age of 16). Incidentally, it is still classified as a crime even if the young female was a willing participant.

The victims of rape

As a behaviour rape is associated with aggression and violence (Holmstrom and Burgess, 1980). As Davison and Neale (1998) point out, it is a myth that young attractive women are the sole victims of rape. Rapists have been known to choose children as young as one and women in their eighties. Of course men can be the victim of rape by other males, especially in prisons. Brewer (2000) cites a TV documentary *Banged up*, in which prisoners talk candidly about their experiences of prisons. One prisoner states:

'Jail sex is rife – that is heterosexual men using other prisoners. They would never think of themselves as homosexual.'

How is 'blame' explained?

There is considerable evidence that many people in society see the victims of rape somehow responsible for their attack (e.g. Fischer, 1986). Judges have been known to make reference to the way in which rape victims were dressed at the time of the attack. For example, 'The young lady in question was wearing a very provocative outfit' – implying that somehow she led the perpetrator on.

Commentary

It seems almost beyond belief that the victims of rape should somehow be responsible for their assaults. So why does this attribution appear so common? One possible explanation was proposed by Lerner (1980), which became known as the 'just world phenomenon'. The idea suggests that society finds it too uncomfortable to believe that a person can experience such atrocities, without somehow deserving what they got. It is, in effect, saying, society finds it easier to accept someone 'invited' the assault, rather than the victim was totally blameless.

Marital rape

As will be seen on pp. 84–5, marital rape was not a crime until 1991. Clearly, it is a complicated allegation to prove, because of the intimate nature of the relationship between husband and wife. In a survey conducted in San Francisco by Russell (1983), it was found that 14 per cent of women who were married (or had been married) had been raped by their husband.

Commentary

Studies have shown a link between marital violence and rape (e.g. Frieze, 1983). Clearly, these relationships were experiencing broader difficulties than just sexual problems. Why would a man wish to rape his wife? Russell (1983) identifies three general areas of explanation:

- anger
- power domination
- sadism.

Men raped by women

It may appear to be a physical impossibility that a man could be raped by a woman. However, studies have shown that men can get an erection in other emotional states than sexual arousal. Sarrel and Masters (1982) illustrated that anger and terror could sometimes produce 'male erectile responses'. Struckman and Johnson (1988) found that 9 per cent (in their sample of date rape victims) were men. Their study highlighted a subtle difference, however, between the types of coercion used for female victims and male. It appeared that the majority of female victims

had been coerced using physical force, whereas males had been coerced using psychological pressure.

Commentary

Other studies have found that males engage in sexual intercourse, not really wishing to participate. Muehlenhard and Cook (1988) found that men often reported feeling 'obliged to have sexual intercourse'. The reasons they gave included:

- They had been seduced.
- Altruistic reasons (they didn't want to hurt the other person's feelings).
- They felt they lacked sexual experience.
- They were drunk.

Date rape

Studies suggest that 'date rape' is an alarmingly common crime (e.g. Koss *et al*, 1988). It can be defined as forcing individuals to engage in sexual intercourse against their will, while on a date. This definition raises a number of issues including:

- How can it be proved that the victim was not a willing participant in the sexual act?
- The fact they were on a date, implies they were initially interested in the other person.

Both these factors in themselves do not excuse the behaviour itself, but it does complicate matters. Bell *et al* (1994) explored participants' opinions to four fictitious rape scenarios (see Key Study 7).

KEY STUDY 7

Researchers: Bell, Kuriloff and Lottes (1994)

Aims: The aim of this study was to assess differences in attribution of blame to the victims in date rape compared with stranger rape.

Method: Male and female college students were asked to read one of four fictitious descriptions of rape. In two of the scenarios the women was raped by a stranger, in the other two they were raped by a date. After they had read one of these scenarios they were asked to assess the amount of blame they attributed to the victim for the rape.

Results: Both male and female participants attributed more blame to victims

---

in date rape than stranger rape (see Figure 4.3). Female participants, however, overall attributed less blame than males.

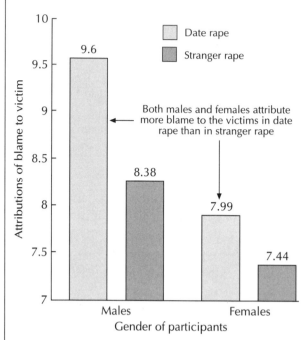

Figure 4.3: Attributions about rape, based upon Bell et al (1994)

Conclusions: Male and female participants differed in their overall levels of attribution of blame. However, both sexes perceived the victim to be more at fault in date rape scenarios than in the stranger rape scenarios.

Commentary

Studies such as Bell *et al's* (1994) highlight two further points:

- Because both males (and to a slightly lesser degree females) tend to hold the victims of date rape responsible for their assault, this may explain why women tend to be more reluctant to report it (Koss and Harvey, 1991).
- Men's greater 'attribution of blame' could account for their higher levels of misinterpretation of female sexual behaviours (Malamuth and Brown, 1994).

As Davison and Neale (1998) graphically point out (by referring to the classic film *Gone with the Wind*):

'Despite initial resistance women like to be taken.'

The date rape drug

Recently, a new development has appeared within the context of date rape, namely the use of a tranquilliser Rohypnol. It is colourless, odourless and tasteless, which makes it an ideal substance to slip into someone's drink (see RLA 16).

Real Life Application 16:

Rohypnol – the date rape drug

Police in Prince William county, Virginia, believe that the drug Rohypnol was used in the rape of two teenage girls. The drug Rohypnol, or 'roofies' as it is known, is a sedative which is said to be ten times as strong as Valium. In medical terms it is a brand name for 'flunitrazepam' (a benzodiazepine sleeping drug). It has no taste or odour which makes it very easy to 'slip into' someone's drink. Amnesia is another effect of the drug, making it difficult to recall the events before and after ingesting it.

In America, the DEA is currently trying to reclassify it as a drug with no medical purpose. It is currently in the same class of drug as marijuana. It's a drug which is still available on private prescription in Britain, however it carries a warning of potential abuse.

Article adapted from KRON – TV Website, 1996

Summary

- American police suspect that the drug Rohypnol was used to rape two girls in 1996.
- Rohypnol is a sedative, has no taste or odour and leaves many of those who have taken it with amnesia.
- At present the drug is still available on private prescription in Britain (2000).

Questions

1 In your own words summarize the features of Rohypnol.

2 Using your knowledge of psychology, give two reasons why individuals might wish to use Rohypnol as a date rape drug.

Historical and cultural factors regarding rape

Matthew Hale, a judge, delivered a ruling in 1736 which stated:

'a husband cannot be guilty of raping his lawful wife'.

His argument was that her marriage contract had given 'implicit consent' to sexual favours, from which she could not retract. This remained the law in England and Wales until 1991, when another judge overturned this ruling saying it was totally inappropriate for modern society.

Perceptions of rape do not only change over time, but culturally as well. Some societies believe that it is through the mixing of semen that conception occurs. For this reason the Merind Anim tribe of New Guinea engage in the gang raping of newly married women (Van Baal, 1966). Clearly, this would be totally unacceptable in modern Western culture, although it is the 'norm' in New Guinea.

Explanations of rape

A question frequently asked by psychologists is, 'Why do individuals rape?'. In a classic study, Gebhard *et al* (1965) suggested that about a third of rapists engaged in this behaviour to express aggression rather than sexual stimulation. Indeed, many feminist commentators see rape as a power-domination phenomenon. The act of rape is less significant than its social consequence, i.e. the debasement of women (Estrich, 1987).

A much more controversial explanation was developed by Thornhill and Wilmsen-Thornhill (1992). They proposed that the evolution of human sexuality is dimorphic (that is, males and females have developed differently). Women tend to assess men for their long-term potential (for the protection of offspring, etc.), whereas men's primary imperative is to impregnate as many females as possible (to increase their chances of fathering offspring). They take this argument further by proposing the 'rape adaptation hypothesis'. By sexually forcing themselves on women, men are increasing their chances of procreating. Rape is an evolutionary adaptive behaviour. More recently this theme has been revisited (see RLA 17).

Real Life Application 17:

Rape makes evolutionary sense!

Want a provocative thesis? Rape is not a crime of violence and power as social scientists tell us – it's motivated by sexual desire and therefore not abnormal!

Thornhill suggests rape is found in other species. He spent many years studying scorpion flies. These are interesting creatures because they have two options when it comes to sexual reproduction. They can either entice the female by offering her gifts of food, then mate with her while she's eating the food, or rape her.

When asked, 'Couldn't this just be a deviant minority of scorpion flies?', he replied:

'I did some experiments showing that all male scorpion flies will switch to raping when they lack a nuptial gift to offer.'

Is there any evidence this hypothesis can be applied to humans?

Thornhill cites a number of pieces of evidence that appear to support his claims. One argument he puts forward is that rapists only use limited violence. He suggests a rapist has to use some violence to achieve his goal, however, if he killed his victim, he would have also killed off any reproductive benefits he had hoped to achieve.

Adapted from an interview with Randy Thornhill in *New Scientist*, 19 February 2000

Summary

- Evolutionary explanations of rape are highly contentious.
- Randy Thornhill (2000) suggests rape is not a crime of violence and power, but a sexual desire by men to spread their genes.
- Even though Thornhill cites a number of ideas that appear to back up his hypothesis, many critics argue it was originally based on flies. Should we generalize to humans?

Questions

1 In your own words, summarize Thornhill's hypothesis.

2 What are the social and ethical implications of his ideas?

Family stress

There are many events which can put a strain on family life. Holmes and Rahe (1967) developed a scale of stressful life events known as the Social Readjustment Rating Scale (SRRS). Their questionnaire measures the level of stress a person is experiencing, by attaching a 'value' or weighting to particular life events. As can be seen in Table 4.3, the values range from 100 points for the death of a spouse to 11 points for minor violations of the law (speeding fines, etc.).

Commentary

There are a number of events which clearly relate directly to family life. Divorce is ranked second, scoring 73 points, closely followed by marital separation, scoring 65 points. Death of a close family member scores 63 points, and marriage scores 50. People score 12 points if it's Christmas – this shouldn't be to surprising since statistics show quarrels and even murders increase during this time (Duck, 1991).

It is usual to get people to check off from the questionnaire the ones that have occurred to them within the last two years. The items are then summed to give a total stress score. Incidentally, single, separated and divorced people reported a larger number of events than married and widowed individuals did (cited by Sarafino, 1990).

We will now go on to highlight four areas of family stress. Firstly, we will consider the impact a new baby can have on the dynamics of a family. Secondly, we will look at illness and the ways in which families cope. Thirdly, on a similar note, we will look at disability and coping, and finally death and bereavement will be considered. Divorce, one of the primary stressors within families, was looked at in detail in Chapter 2 (see p. 47).

A new baby in the family

Even though for most families the birth of a baby is a joyous event, it can bring tremendous stress. The pregnancy and subsequent birth can be stressful for the mother (having to go through the event) but also for the father (at times feeling very helpless) (Shapiro, 1987). The majority of research into childbirth experiences have (not surprisingly) focused on the mother; however, fathers experience stress also. Many worry about increased pressures on finance, whether they will make good fathers and how their relationship with their partner will change (May, 1986).

The baby's temperament

Once the baby is home, it has to be integrated into the existing family unit. The ease of this process partly depends on the temperament (infantile personality characteristics) of the child. Psychologists have documented temperaments for many years, suggesting there are 'easy and difficult' varieties (Buss and Plomin, 1975). Indeed, studies have

Table 4.3: The Social Readjustment Rating Scale, based on Holmes and Rahe (1967) from the Journal of Psychosomatic Research, *11, pp. 213–18, copyright 1967, with permission from Elsevier Science*

Rank	Life event	Mean value
1	Death of spouse	100
2	Divorce	73
3	Marital separation	65
4	Jail term	63
5	Death of close family member	63
6	Personal injury or illness	53
7	Marriage	50
8	Fired at work	47
9	Marital reconciliation	45
10	Retirement	45
11	Change in health of family member	44
12	Pregnancy	40
13	Sex difficulties	39
14	Gain of new family member	39
15	Business readjustment	39
16	Change in financial state	38
17	Death of a close friend	37
18	Change to different line of work	36
19	Change in number of arguments with spouse	35
20	Mortgage over US $10,000	31
21	Foreclosure of mortgage or loan	30
22	Change in responsibilities at work	29
23	Son or daughter leaving home	29
24	Trouble with in-laws	29
25	Outstanding personal achievement	28
26	Wife begins or stops work	26
27	Begin or end school	26
28	Change in living conditions	25
29	Revision of personal habits	24
30	Trouble with boss	23
31	Change in work hours or conditions	20
32	Change in residence	20
33	Change in schools	20
34	Change in recreation	19
35	Change in church activities	19
36	Change in social activities	18
37	Mortgage or loan less than US $10,000	17
38	Change in sleeping habits	16
39	Change in number of family get-togethers	15
40	Change in eating habits	15
41	Vacation	13
42	Christmas	12
43	Minor violations of the law	11

demonstrated that 'difficult temperaments' can be very stressful to parents (Cutrona and Troutman, 1986).

The effect on siblings

It is not only the parents who have to adjust to the arrival of a new member of the family, siblings have to as well. Research has shown it can be a very stressful time for them (Honig, 1987). Levels of stress appear to be worse, the younger the child.

Clearly, jealously towards the newborn and feelings of insecurity are contributing factors here. A younger child is more needy than an older one.

Commentary

This concept of sibling rivalry has been taken to a new dimension in recent years with the publication of a book entitled *PsychoDarwinism* (Badcock, 1994). In it, Badcock attempts to link Freudian concepts to Darwinian theory. He discusses Freud's oral phase of psychosexual development in which a baby engages in suckling behaviour to experience sexual pleasure. He argues this behaviour has an evolutionary benefit – as breast-feeding acts as a form of contraception (though not a reliable one). This would mean a child who engaged in plenty of breast-feeding behaviour reduces the chances of his or her mother getting pregnant immediately. The child would be reducing its chances of having a rival at the breast. In a similar way, Freud believed that young children obtain sexual feelings from withholding their faeces. From a Darwinian point of view, a mother would direct food to her most needy offspring. If a child was not defecating (by deliberately holding it in), a mother may increase that child's supply of food. The more resources it obtained, the better its chances of survival.

Illness

Illness is usually defined as acute (short lived) or chronic (long term). When members of a family fall ill, it can create difficulties and stress. However, in the majority of cases the illness is usually short lived, and apart from causing inconvenience, the family deals with it and soon returns to normal. However, chronic illness brings with it different problems.

Illness in adults

When adults develop chronic illness, often the family's interpersonal relationships change (Michela, 1987). Fear regarding the course of the illness, or worries over finance, all contribute to the levels of stress experienced. The age of the family member is also important. As Leventhal *et al* (1985) point out:

'Cancer in an 80-year-old woman has quite a different meaning than the same disease in a 30-year-old woman with two young children.'

Illness in children

Chronic illness in children is especially difficult, because apart from the long-term adaptations which have to be made (Johnson, 1985), the psychological adjustments also have a considerable impact. Parents often feel a sense of loss (of not having a healthy child), and often feel 'cheated' in terms of the time they can spend together. Also, siblings may feel isolated and deprived of parental attention (Sarafino, 1994).

Breslau *et al* (1981) looked at siblings of children suffering from a range of disabilities from birth, including cerebral palsy. They found that there was a significant difference in levels of aggression of these children to their peers. Children who had sick brothers or sisters tended to be more aggressive to other children. Breslau assumed feelings of neglect (because of their sibling's condition) manifested themselves in aggression and antisocial behaviour.

Disability

Many studies on disability have focused upon the carers of the disabled person. Research has shown that the stress on families can be severe if an individual needs constant assistance, and they have mental deterioration as well (Robinson and Thurnher, 1986). Looking after a family member, washing them, dressing them, feeding them can be hard enough, but knowing they are not aware of your efforts can be soul destroying.

Disability and sexual relationships

Disabled people frequently get labelled as not being able to do anything. Just because someone is in a wheelchair, it does not make him or her incapable of sexual behaviour. Indeed, the majority of disabled people are able to lead active and healthy sexual lives. As Milton Diamond (1992) puts it:

'… the brain is the most sexy organ of all. It is the total person and not the genital region alone, that makes sexual response meaningful and special.'

Commentary

For some disabled people, however, the opportunities to engage in sexual relationships are very limited. An American social worker Harvey Gochros describes the deliberate 'blocking' of disabled people to engage in sexual behaviour as 'sexual oppression' (Gochros *et al*, 1986). Society marginalizes certain groups, not encouraging them to enter the sexual arena.

Bereavement

As we saw earlier on the Social Readjustment Rating Scale (Holmes and Rahe, 1967), death of a spouse and family member are both in the top five stressful life events. It is no wonder that their effects within the family unit can be dramatic. Bereavement affects more than 800,000 people each year in the USA alone. Studies have shown that young children under 5 appear to grieve for a lost parent less, and recover more quickly than an adolescent (Rutter, 1983). It is suggested that due to their cognitive immaturity they do not fully understand the implications of what has happened. By about the age of 8, most children are able to understand that death is not a temporary change. Adjusting to family life without having both parents around is what makes death so stressful.

Death of a child

Arguably, the worst thing that can befall parents is the loss of their child. Edelstein (1984) points out not only is it a loss of a person, but also a symbolic loss for the parents' hopes and aspirations for the future.

Relationship therapies

As we have already seen in Chapter 2, relationships break down for many reasons. There are a variety of sources of help available other than 'the professionals' (counsellors, psychologists and psychiatrists). In the early part of the twentieth century in Britain, communities tended to be much more 'close knit', often with friends and members of the same family living a few doors away. This gave the opportunity for people to talk about their problems (for more information on this see p. 88). One organization, which has over 50 years' experience counselling couples with relationship problems is Relate. RLA 19 looks at Relate's aims and identifies some of the problems it deals with.

Real Life Application 18:

Relate – the couples counselling agency

Relate is Britain's leading couple counselling agency. It is a national charity with over 50 years' experience of helping partners. It provides three main services:

- counselling – couples or one to one
- sex therapy – couples or individuals who have specific sexual problems
- education and training – a range of training programmes presented to individuals or groups.

Usually counselling sessions are once a week for an hour. The same counsellor is seen each time.

Staff are carefully selected and given training (to nationally recognized standards). All counsellors receive continued support and supervision, and are trained to refer to other professionals where necessary.

Clients are expected to pay according to their income. This is negotiated at the first session.

Summary

- Relate is Britain's largest couple counselling charity.
- It provides counselling, sex therapy and education and training programmes.
- Counsellors are trained to nationally recognized standards, and receive continued support and supervision.

Questions

1 Identify the key features of Relate.

2 Assess the contribution Relate provides to society.

Couples therapy

Davison and Neale (1998) point out that until quite recently, couples therapy used to be referred to as marital therapy. However, with the growing numbers of people who now 'cohabit' (be that opposite sex or same-sex couples), it is more useful to regard them as 'couples'.

Underlying rationale

The idea of this type of therapy is to modify the interactions of two people who are in conflict with one another. A trained therapist establishes a therapeutic contract with the couple and works with them on maladaptive patterns of behaviour. There are distinctions between 'couples therapy' and 'couples counselling' (Kaplan and Sadock, 1994). Counselling (as used by Relate) tends to be primarily task-orientated, attempting to solve specific problems – such as organization of money or child-rearing issues. Therapy, on the other hand, focuses on the underlying issues within the relationship. This could include exploring the psychodynamics of each partner (based on Freudian concepts), it could involve changing the behaviours of the couple or it could involve analysing the emotional security of each partner (emotion focused therapy). Let's take each of these in turn, and look at them in more detail.

A psychodynamic approach

A common Freudian idea is that we use our mother as 'the prototype of all later loving relationships'. If a man therefore has some 'deep-seated' unconscious frustration about the relationship he had with his mother (as a baby), he may well make excessive, even infantile demands upon his current partner. Making him aware of this fact can lead to a better understanding by the couple. Fitzgerald (1973), in his book *Conjoint marital therapy*, talks about the transference that exists (within the therapeutic relationship) between the two partners. He suggests a major focus of the therapist should be to get couples to see each other as 'individuals', rather than symbolic mother or father figures.

Commentary

One of the major problems with psychodynamic approaches to therapy is that they are based upon Freudian theory. Many commentators have consistently attacked this work for its unscientific and ineffective nature (e.g. Eysenck, 1952, 1992). In many ways, knowing that your current relationship is failing because of parental relationship problems in early childhood is not a lot of use, because 'the damage' has already been done.

A cognitive-behavioural approach

As you might expect, cognitive-behavioural treatments focus on the behaviours couples engage in, and the thinking that underpins them. Stuart (1976) developed an interesting technique (based on operant conditioning principles) in which he got one partner to carry out a number of 'nice things' for the other on one particular day, and got the other partner to do the same on a subsequent day. If the couple 'stuck to the deal' they would experience positive reinforcement (for a fuller explanation of this see p. 22). Even though these experiences were 'artificially coerced' initially, Stuart argued that after a while they would become natural, and part of the couple's repertoire. Cognitive-behavioural approaches also adopt ideas from Thiabaut and Kelley's (1959) exchange theory (see Chapter 1, p. 24). Couples are encouraged to analyse their relationships, in an attempt to discover what each is giving and receiving.

Commentary

Does the research literature provide evidence that 'meeting the needs of partners' in an equitable way, produces relationship happiness? Certainly, Wood and Jacobson (1985) suggest that the subjective quality of a relationship can be judged on the relative rates of pleasant and unpleasant interactions. Also, there has been a growing trend within behaviour therapy as a whole to incorporate more cognitive aspects (Baucom *et al*, 1995). This is particularly true in couples therapy where it is vital to understand the way in which people attribute blame.

An emotion-focused approach

A specific approach has been developed by therapists such as Alexander *et al* (1994) and is referred to as emotionally focused therapy (EFT). As the name implies it concentrates upon the feelings of the couple, and in particular the importance of basic instincts such as a need for protection, security and belongingness (Johnson and Greenberg, 1995).

Commentary

We met this concept in Chapter 1 when we looked at Maslow's Hierarchy of Needs model (see p. 3). This approach suggests that if an individual perceives his or her relationship to be failing in its role of providing a 'secure base', it will lead to distress and dysfunction. EFT attempts to correct this situation.

Family therapy

One of the obvious differences between couples therapy and family therapy is that the latter involves working with all members of the family. In most cases this involves parents and children. Family therapy as a method of clinical psychology started in the 1960s and has continued to develop ever since.

Techniques used in family therapy

The interview process is of paramount importance to both couples therapy and family therapy. The therapist needs to 'facilitate the sessions', bearing two important facts in mind

- The family comes to therapy with its dynamics already in place. Often this can be the most important presenting problem, over and above specific difficulties.
- More often than not families cohabit, so are, to some degree, dependent upon one another. Any analysis within a session has to take into account this interdependence.

Virginia Satir (1967) developed the Family-Life Chronology technique. It was proposed as a way of opening up 'productive dialogue' and acts as a frame-work to build therapy upon.

There are other techniques used apart from working with just one family. In 'family group therapy', therapists combine several families into a single group, and work with them on shared issues. One (not always obvious benefit) of group work is that families come to realize they are not alone with a particular problem. It can be both comforting and informative to be in the company of fellow 'sufferers'.

Applications of family therapy

The academic literature is littered with studies that assess therapeutic interventions within a family setting. Let us consider two such examples.

Stratton and Swaffer (1988) used family therapy to help mothers who were physically abusing their children. They recorded the attributions that mothers gave to their children's behaviour, and compared them with those of 'normal' and physically disabled children, all of similar socio-economic background. They found that the attributions made by the mothers who were abusing their children were significantly different. They perceived their children's behaviour to be less controllable. These findings allowed them to develop a programme to help guide the mothers' 'cognitions' and to develop strategies to help them cope with their perceived uncontrollability.

Alexander and Parsons (1973) undertook family therapy, using delinquent adolescents. The programme involved using modelling and reinforcement techniques to 're-shape' the way in which family members interacted with one another. They compared this type of treatment with three others. In the first condition the boys only met with their social worker as normal (no treatment group). In the second, they met their social worker regularly but had no formal structured intervention (family group). The third group was exposed to fairly eclectic psychodynamic interventions (the psychodynamic group). They assessed the success of the programme by looking at the 'recidivism rate' over time (that is the rate of repeat offending). They found that the behaviour modification group performed the best (see Figure 4.4).

Commentary

Cognitive-behavioural interventions appear to work well when dealing with delinquency within the family. Studies such as the two outlined above illustrate the usefulness of involving the 'whole family' in therapy.

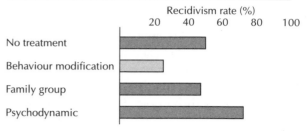

Non-treatment control group	50%
Behaviour modification	**26%**
Family group, unstructured contact	47%
Eclèctic psychodynamic family group programme	73%

Figure 4.4: Recidivism rates of delinquent adolescents after family-based therapy, based on Alexander and Parsons from the Journal of Abnormal Psychology, *1973, 81, 219–225. Copyright © 1973 by the American Psychological Association. Reprinted with permission.*

SECTION 2

Loneliness

As we defined earlier in this chapter, loneliness is a 'forced social isolation', whereas solitude is a matter of choice. Psychologists have studied the effects of loneliness over many years. However, loneliness is not a concept which is straightforward to understand. An individual could live in a flat on his or her own, but have a 'high power job', allowing for many social interactions during the day. He or she could go to many parties and enjoy the company of others. However, psychologically the individual could be lonely. Duck (1992) attempts to explain this phenomenon by pointing out that social interactions are all about 'quality' not 'quantity'. The individual in our example clearly had many interactions, but none of them meaningful. So what is it about meaningful relationships which does us good?

Social support

Many psychologists point to the fact that being with others provides 'social support'. Cobb and Jones (1984) suggest social support can be considered along three dimensions:

1 Actual supportive behaviour of friends and family.
2 The nature of an individual's social network (whether it is more communal or more individualistic).
3 The way the person feels about the social support he or she receives.

Argyle (1987) argues that married people or those living with a partner have the best social support.

He goes on to suggest that it acts as a 'buffer' against a variety of 'life changes'. One area of 'life change' that has been extensively studied is loneliness in non-working mothers, with young children. Brown and Harris (1978) found four factors which pre-disposed women to depression. They included having several young children and not having paid employment outside the home. Clearly, stress and loneliness were contributing to depression.

House clearance and its effects on community

There have been a number of studies and books written about the effects of slum housing clearance programmes on communities (e.g. Dowson, 1997; Jennings, 1962; Ungerson, 1971). All of them stress the need for better housing, but point out that communities were 'split up' and sent to new modern houses in different parts of the towns and cities. Focal points of communities (such as pubs and working men's clubs) were demolished to make way for city centre shops. Prior to the mid 1960s the main objective of slum clearance was rehousing families, particularly young ones. There was little consideration for social interaction (Dowson, 2000). In many cases this fragmentation of existing communities led to isolation and loneliness. The chat over the backyard fence, or the helping hand from the neighbour across the road had been severely curtailed (see RLA 19).

Real Life Application 19:
Neighbourhood loneliness

Material A – a case study of Middlesbrough
Dowson (1997) conducted an in-depth study of 'slum housing clearance' in an inner city area of Middlesbrough, during the 1960s. He interviewed 20 ex-residents from the Wilson-Hill Street district of Middlesbrough, and collected biographic recollections of their feelings at the time. What was evident from his findings was a total exclusion of social and amenity features in the planning submissions for the Wilson-Hill Street clearance. In their rush to create 'modern' housing the planners 'forgot about community'. Many of those interviewed felt a sense of shock and isolation when they witnessed their old neighbourhood being 'pulled down'.

Article adapted from Dowson, unpublished PhD thesis, 1997

Material B – loneliness in present-day society
A headline in *The Guardian* (2000) posed the question, 'Are we turning into a nation of loners?'. The article went on to point out Britain is entering a period of change in which adults lead more isolated lives. More than 6.5 million people in Britain now live on their own. This accounts for about 28 per cent of households. This is three times more than forty years ago.

Article adapted from *The Guardian*, 27 March 2000.

Summary

- Studies have shown that slum housing clearance fragmented neighbourhoods, mainly because planners focused upon the quality of housing rather than community.
- Dowson (1997) found participants felt a sense of shock and isolation when their neighbourhood was pulled down.
- Statistics show that our present society is becoming more 'lonely'. Twenty-eight per cent of households live on their own, a threefold increase in the past forty years.

Questions

1 Using your psychological knowledge, give some reasons as to how 'neighbourhoods' can help reduce loneliness.

2 Give two reasons why more people live on their own today than 40 years ago.

Relationships and electronic media

Let us now turn our attention to another contemporary issue. The use of electronic media has mushroomed within the past ten years. One of the largest growth areas within this field has been the Internet. It is unknown just how many people are connected to the World Wide Web, but estimations range from about 35 million to 40 million. A survey in the *1997 World Fact Book* (Central Intelligence Agency), showed 15% of the population of the USA were Internet users in 1997, a figure predicted to rise to 53% by 2001. In the UK, over 50% of Internet users use e-mail to stay in touch with friends (BRMB International, January 1999). Clearly, individuals are able to 'talk' with one another more than ever before. But this is not face-to-face communication.

Commentary

Some commentators have suggested making friends on the Internet is 'an easy option, because you don't have to meet them in the flesh!' (Kingston, 2000). Even more cynically, in 1997 *The Guardian* announced 'Net addicts lead sad virtual lives'. The article went on to look at the lives of people who spend hours a day 'surfing the net'. It is no wonder we find statistics such as the ones identified in RLA 19 (material B). The Internet appears to have reduced our need for 'physical social contact'. Writing a letter has been replaced by using a keyboard and a screen, and waiting a week for a reply has been replaced by almost instant responses. So what are the psychological implications of these new technologies?

The psychology of the Internet

People who use the Internet exist in what is referred to as 'cyberspace'. They communicate with others throughout the world using a variety of facilities including 'e-mail, electronic discussion groups and bulletin boards', to name but a few. They are anonymous (usually only known by a username chosen by the individual) and are for the most part undetectable (in terms of their geographical location). As Angus Kennedy, author of the best selling *The Internet – the rough guide* (2000) puts it, this distance and anonymity often makes for 'startlingly intimate communication'. The idea that people's behaviour changes depending on proximity and anonymity is well illustrated by studies into obedience and aggression.

The effects of proximity on behaviour

Stanley Milgram (1963) conducted a study into obedience by requesting participants to administer what they believed to be real electric shocks to stooges (confederates of the experimenter). One interesting result of the study was that the proximity of the participant to the stooge affected the level of obedience. When they were in separate rooms, obedience levels (to administer the shock) were high. When the participant and stooge were in the same room (placed about one and a half feet apart) the obedience level dropped to about 40 per cent. There was a further drop (to 30 per cent) when the participants were requested to hold stooges' hands down on the 'shock plate'. If the researcher left the room altogether the levels of obedience dropped to about 20.5 per cent. When the experimenter gave instructions over the phone (to administer the shock), participants frequently pretended to administer it, or they disobeyed and reduced the voltage.

Commentary

Milgram's (1963) study illustrates that people tend to adapt their behaviour, depending on the influence closest to them (in terms of proximity). It is almost like a process of regression has taken place and people become naughty children, being most naughty when they don't think anyone can see them. In Milgram's work, when the researcher was standing next to them, and the stooge was in another room, the participants were more likely to obey the researcher's instructions. When the stooge was in the room with the participant and the researcher was on the other end of a telephone, on the whole the participants felt a high level of concern and acted 'in line' with their conscience. In relationship terms it is often easier to discuss difficult issues or behave in certain ways when we are 'distanced' from the other person, than when we are face to face. Kennedy (2000) points out that the Internet allows people to reinvent themselves, but goes on to warn:

'… if you find yourself in private counsel with a "Prince", don't swoon too soon. After all, on the Internet no one can tell if you're a dog'.

The effects of 'deindividuation'

In theories of aggression the concept of deindividuation has been used in an attempt to explain why people 'act out of character' when they feel they are anonymous. When an individual's identity is lost (perhaps by being part of a much larger group) or facets of his or her personality are blurred (perhaps by taking drugs) the person is said to be individuated (Gergen and Gergen, 1981). A classic study into this phenomenon was conducted by Diener *et al* (1976). In a large-scale observation on Hallowe'en night, they found that children playing 'trick or treat' were more likely to become involved in petty crime (stealing money or sweets) if they were wearing costumes, masks, etc., and their identity was hidden. By believing they cannot be identified, individuals' behaviour potentially becomes less 'censored'.

Commentary

Both these examples highlight issues that can easily relate to Internet relationships. Perhaps they suggest people will be more likely to behave 'out of character' online than they would face to face. A person may say things via e-mail, that they may be reluctant to say 'in the flesh'. Embarrassment, inhibition and fear of rejection are more powerful in a real life scenario than they are in cyberspace. Arguably a benefit of communications such as e-mail is that they appear to reduce status differences between people (Dubrovsky *et al*, 1991).

Whatever the advantages and disadvantages (depending on how you view them) of Internet communication, statistics illustrate that it is on the increase. But why should people want to engage in it? RLA 20 gives one potential answer. It illustrates the role the Internet can have in providing a 'virtual' community or neighbourhood. As we saw in RLA 19, the concept of neighbourhood appears to be important. Maybe 'talking on the net' is equivalent to the original chat over the backyard fence.

Real Life Application 20:
A virtual neighbourhood

A 'surfer' explains that for him the computer is an extension of the pub. When he gets home and 'logs on' he makes a neat transition from chatting to someone in the pub to chatting to someone in cyberspace. The Internet allows people to 'post' their thoughts on particular issues, and others to read and respond to them. Often conversations can 'drift on for months'. An interesting feature of communicating in cyberspace is that people are far more candid and honest, than perhaps they would be in real life. Friends made over the 'net' become to an individual, 'a virtual neighbourhood'.

Adapted from article by Jim McClellan, *The Observer*, 13 February 1994.

Summary

- The Internet acts as a 'meeting place' to share thoughts, feelings and ideas.
- People communicate in candid and honest ways.
- Cyberspace has become for many, a 'virtual neighbourhood'.

Questions

1 What are the advantages and disadvantages of using the Internet to communicate, rather than talking to a person face to face?

2 Identify four 'chat room' addresses on the Internet, and summarize what their main functions are.

Human relationships with information technology

The concept of computers being user friendly was arguably first coined by Kogon *et al* (1977) when they identified '... a growing trend to user friendly systems'. The term caught on and now 'user friendly' has become second nature to most of us. However, Simons (1985) suggests this term should disturb us, because it suggests that the specifically human attribute friendliness – can be attributed to machines.

Information technology – the 'marriage wrecker'

The idea of machines acting as 'substitute humans' was taken to its extreme in a case reported in *The Guardian* in November 1983. A mini-cab driver described his remarkable affair with a personal computer (PC). He became obsessed with the PC he used, feeling jealous when others used it, and asking it questions such as 'Do you love me?' – to which it always replied yes (he had programmed it to respond this way). When the PC was eventually taken away for a more up-to-date model, he was broken-hearted and in his despair, started to loath everything to do with computers. His loss had made him a bitter and twisted man. What makes this case even more remarkable was that his wife believed he was having an affair (with a woman), and he was forced to leave his wife and two sons. A computer had broken up a marriage. Clearly, this is an extreme case. However, there is more evidence that information technology can wreck marriages.

Rossman (1983) wrote an article entitled 'Of marriage in the computing age' in which he cites Mary and Kevin, a couple experiencing marital difficulties because of Kevin's obsession with his computer. After making love with Mary, Kevin would get up and start working on the computer. Rossman cites a perceptive observation by an American relationship therapist, Marcia Perlstein:

'Computer involvement tends to be compellingly hypnotic, as addictive as a drug. It can be worse than another lover as a competing force for attention.'

So as we move forward in the twenty-first century, the increase in computer usage appears to be a worrying prospect for our interpersonal relationships. Perhaps we would do well to remember, just as when we write a letter, or use the telephone, it's not the medium itself we are having the relationship with, but the person at the other end.

Gay men and the Internet

We have already seen in Chapter 3 that homosexual relationships are still relatively marginalized. Often, gay men find it difficult to meet other gay men, and so many rely on 'doing the gay scene' (which involves gay bars, cafes, clubs, etc.). The Internet provides another opportunity to 'talk with' and meet like-minded men. David Shaw (1997) has conducted research in this area. Key Study 8 details this work.

KEY STUDY 8

Researcher: Shaw (1997)

Aim: The aim of the research was to identify the experiences 'gay men' had of using an Internet 'chat system'.

Method: Detailed interviews with 12 gay men, who used Internet Relay Chat (IRC), a system where you can chat in text or audio to others in real time, was conducted.

Results: He found that Internet interactions led to:
'... a mixed bag of excitement and disgust, promise and letdown, nonchalance and embarrassment'.
Just like life it was perhaps the 'rich mix' which made this form of communication so appealing.

Conclusions: Shaw concluded that unlike much of the previous criticism of 'surfers' being lonely, sad individuals who are scared to meet:
'... all of the men actively transgressed the bounds of bodilessness through the exchange of GIFs, photographs, phone calls and ultimately face-to-face'
(which Shaw saw as their main objective).

Sex in a 'Cyber society'

For some individuals the experience of sex in the real world is either lacking or falling short of expectations. Technology has now delivered virtual sex where everything seems to be happening but in reality nothing ever does.

Virtual sex is the latest form of computer-generated technology to enable people to escape their physical natural world into a world of make-believe and assumed identities. Warwick (1994), a professor in Cybernetics at Reading University, claims that:

'Robot intelligence resembling that of humans will be around within the next 50 years – they could also have the human sexual responses "wired in" as well.'

Relationships with animals

History is full of accounts of human relationships with animals. Case studies of 'feral children' litter the scientific and fictional literature. What are feral children? Definitions vary, but literally speaking a feral child is one that is 'wild' or existing in a state of nature (Reber, 1985). Perhaps the best known scientific case study of a feral child was Victor, the wild boy of Aveyron. He was discovered in 1800, in southern France, and had been living wild, existing on a diet of acorns and stolen potatoes. Even though there was no scientific evidence that Victor had been raised by animals, the locals believed due to his mannerisms and vocalizations (he couldn't actually speak) that he had been raised by wolves. Perhaps the best known literary example of a feral child is Edgar Rice Burrough's character, Tarzan, who was orphaned as a baby, and discovered and raised by apes. There is much scientific debate as to whether this would be possible in 'real life'.

Pets as promoters of health

Regardless of whether it is possible to be 'nurtured' by members of another species, scientists are sure of one thing, and that is, living with pet animals can benefit physical and psychological health. The Ancient Greeks thought that human diseases could be cured if the afflicted part of the body was licked by a dog – however, they did believe that dogs were 'gods' in disguise. In Elizabethan times, physicians suggested that women could benefit from holding 'lapdogs', 'as they would absorb diseases emanating from other people' (cited by Martin, 1997). In more recent times, modern science has begun to endorse the benefits of 'pet owning'.

Relationships between pets and humans – the current view

Most of the current literature on pet owning and

health refers to pets as 'companion animals'. For lonely individuals, or people who are socially isolated, a companion animal can provide interaction, conversation and thought that would otherwise not exist (Totman, 1990). Apart from these psychological benefits, a vast wealth of studies has illustrated physical benefits. An interesting piece of research conducted by Erika Friedman *et al* (1980), and published in a volume of Public Health reports, found that the death rate for heart attack victims, a year after their initial attack, was five times lower if they owned pets, compared to those who did not. Interestingly, it did not appear to make any difference what type of pet it was – so the argument that dog owners take more exercise did not seem to apply.

Research has found that stroking pets can reduce blood pressure. One study found that participants' blood pressure was slightly reduced to the exposure of a mild stressor, when their companion animals were allowed to be present (cited by Ornstein and Sobel, 1988).

The relationship owners have with their pets has been viewed by some academics as so important that they have suggested that 'death of a companion animal' should be added to the scale of stressful life events among the elderly (Lazarus, 1988).

Commentary

Clearly, the strong attachment bond that forms between an owner and an animal companion is responsible for providing many of these positive health effects. Ornstein and Sobel (1988) suggested that pets provide owners with a sense of purpose and responsibility. It is this feeling of being needed and wanted that enhances physiological functioning. But evidence also suggests, owning a more conventional pet can also enhance an individual's chance of meeting new people (see RLA 21).

Real Life Application 21:

Walking the dog – 'a good social exercise'

Recent research evidence has shown that owning a dog can increase an individual's chance of initiating social interaction. McNicholas *et al* (2000) from Warwick University conducted a study in which she and colleagues took part. They demonstrated that no matter what guise (scruffy or smart) or whether you are male or female, being in the presence of a dog will encourage people to interact with you. Her team concludes:

'Dogs are good ice-breakers.'

It appears that this theory works in real life, even in the lives of celebrities. Host of the popular TV show *Don't try this at home*, Davina McCall, recently admitted in an interview that she met her husband while out walking her dog.

Article adapted from *New Scientist*, 19 February 2000.

Summary

- Evidence suggests being in the presence of a dog increases social interaction.
- McNicholas *et al* (2000) found this result to be consistent regardless of the researcher's appearance (smart or scruffy) or their sex.
- As Davina McCall testifies, walking a dog can provide an excellent 'ice-breaker', even help finding a future partner.

Questions

1 What type of research design did McNicholas *et al* use?

2 In what ways do you think the presence of a dog facilitates social interaction?

Essay questions

1 a Outline and evaluate some potential problems with domestic relationships.

  b In what ways can psychology help to alleviate these problems?

2 Evolutionary theories suggest that 'homo sapiens' (humans) are social animals. To what extent is this true?

3 In what ways has research into Western contemporary issues helped to inform psychologists about the diversity in interpersonal relationships?

A Advice on answering essay questions

Chapter 1

1 This question requires you to describe a range of explanations as to why humans are social beings. It would be a good idea to start with the evolutionary and biological perspectives, discussing ideas such as co-operation. Psychological theories must be considered, including need fulfilment and reinforcement.

2 This question is asking you to look at different explanations of how friendships form. Assessing a broad range of theories would be the most sensible approach here. You are asked specifically to consider the process, so explanations of balance theory, reinforcement theory and economic concepts would be important.

3 It would be appropriate to start by giving some examples of evolutionary explanations of relationships. Throughout Chapter 1 we considered the disadvantages of evolutionary models. You need to incorporate these into your answer. Remember evolutionary models do not cope well with individual, social or cultural differences.

Chapter 2

1 This question is asking you to look specifically at relationship breakdown (referred to as dissolution – so don't get caught out!). You need to identify processes and factors that have been shown to contribute to breakdown – e.g. by considering the opposite perspective of attraction and looking at the work of Steve Duck.

2a This part of the question requires you to look at theories of how and why relationships 'start' in the first place. You can consider prior expectations and factors of attraction. Remember you need to look at the advantages and disadvantages of each theory.

2b The second part is asking you to do very much the same as in part 2a, except by focusing on breakdown. Again evaluations are needed of the theories.

3 This is a very straightforward question, requiring you to identify theories and factors which have been shown to affect attraction. It's important to make some assessment regarding their 'usefulness'. Better answers will address the question of 'What is beauty?' by considering cross-cultural and historical perspectives.

4 The content of this essay will be predominantly the same as question 2. Remember that critical analysis must be given, which you will find frequently appearing in the commentary sections.

Chapter 3

1 Philosophically, this is a very difficult question to answer, however practically it is more straightforward. You are asked to identify how psychologists have attempted to explain love, so theories must be identified and assessed. This could include excitation theory and studies that have looked at cultural and sex differences regarding love.

2 This question needs you to set the scene by discussing the concept of marriage – you could even include evolutionary ideas of 'pair-bonding' here. Then perceptions of marriage from other cultures need to be explored and evaluated. As the essay is posing a question, you need to end with an answer. Is marriage a 'socially constructed concept'?

3 This question invites you to look at research into homosexual relationships, but it requires you to do more than this. It requires a comparison with heterosexual relationships. For example, how can homosexuals publicly demonstrate their attachment to one another? How are roles defined in domestic life?

Chapter 4

1a This question invites you to look at domestic problems. These could include violence, rape, disharmony and divorce. You need to explain the impact these problems have on society and the individuals concerned.

1b This part of the question is asking you to suggest ways in which psychology can intervene in domestic problems. You could mention studies which specifically suggest how improvements can be made (e.g. changes in law, etc.), also you could focus on therapy. Here you would need to explain how the therapies attempt to help and how effective they are.

2 This is a difficult question to answer, because it challenges a widely held assumption. However, you could look at isolated religious orders and hermits, and explain the role of 'attachment to God' as an alternative to humans.

3 You would need to start this essay by identifying specific contemporary issues, e.g. 'gay couples adopting' or families living in communes. Using these, you could go on to look at how theories have evolved regarding 'alternative lifestyles'. You would need to conclude by suggesting that this has shown psychologists that there is no such thing as the 'archetypal relationship'.

A Advice on answering short answer questions

Chapter 1

RLA 1

1 Karen and Brian.

2 Fiona.

3 Between Lucy and Mike, and Mike and Brian.

RLA 2

1 A chemical substance used as a means of communication between members of a species.

2 We are a higher level species and that means we rely on 'cognitive feedback' regarding others, not 'animal-like' smells. Also, we could mask our natural body odours by wearing personal hygiene products such as after-shave and perfume.

RLA 3

1 You must summarize using your own words.

2 Yes. When children are very young they require nurture themselves. Cuddly toys would provide them with 'contact comfort'. As they get older children start to develop nurturing behaviours themselves – these are often directed at their cuddly toys.

RLA 4

1 Harlow's work suggests that 'cuddling' is a primitive behaviour which could therefore be added to Maslow's Hierarchy of Needs. It is debatable at which level it could be added – you could make the point it appeared to be as important as feeding for Harlow's monkeys.

2 Mothers can recognize offspring by touch alone. Touch has been shown to benefit premature babies' physiology. Touch makes humans feel loved and special.

RLA 5

1 It is always assumed that men are more promis-cuous than women because of their uncertainty regarding their paternity. However, Pento-Voak's ideas suggest that women have a sexual strategy also. They choose 'softer-looking' men to nurture their children, while choosing more 'rugged men' to reproduce with.

2 Contrary to general opinion women are just as promiscuous as men, but they are perhaps less obvious.

Chapter 2

RLA 6

1 Lowey conducted research using fashion models – they are chosen because of specific features. Only specific features were investigated – they were taken out of context.

2 If there is a formula to the 'perfect look' and it proves to be universal by being cross-cultural, it suggests that there is an evolutionary advantage to those who possess these features.

RLA 7

1 37 per cent (out of the eight males, three specifically state a younger age range).

2 87 per cent of females (seven out of eight use positive descriptions). They include statements such as: slim and attractive.
87 per cent of males (seven out of eight use positive descriptions). They include statements such as: professional, slim, and tall.

3 50 per cent (four out of eight) of the males; none of the females.

4 62 per cent of males state their height exactly, 25 per cent of males make no reference to their height.

RLA 8

1 An irrational emotional state in which a person lacks a feeling of security with a beloved partner.

2 Firstly, health care professionals are recognizing symptoms more readily, therefore referring more clients. Secondly, contemporary relationships are becoming less stable, leading potentially to more cases of jealousy.

Chapter 3

RLA 9

1 One idea could be that in public, it shows who you 'wish' to be seen to be close to.

2 By seeing it as an evolutionary behaviour, there is a tendency to miss the importance of the social and cultural aspects of kissing.

RLA 10

1 Zulus seem to value 'young love' as the instigator of marriage. However, young couples have to abide by many strict rules of conduct when expressing their love for one another. Also, remember, the 'pool' of potential partners they have to choose from is relatively small.

2 The first stage could be seen as 'going out with one another. The second stage might equate to parental approval. The third stage is engagement, where the couple's intentions are made public. Fourthly, the wedding ceremony takes place where family and friends are invited to eat and drink.

RLA 11

1 Arguably, different cultures have different views on polygamy. Marriage is a widely accepted way in which individuals demonstrate publicly their emotional attachment to one another.

2 *Pros* – increases the likelihood of children and allows for less intense relationships. *Cons* – leads to jealousy and a lack of feeling special.

RLA 12

1 You must summarize using your own words.

2 *Pros* – it would show researchers that something as complex as human sexual behaviour can be controlled by genes. Also, it could illustrate to homophobics that homosexuality is as natural as having blue or brown eyes. *Cons* – it may lead some to suggest that homosexuality is a genetic abnormality. A screening test could be developed to identify sexual orientation. In the 'wrong hands' this could encourage discrimination.

Chapter 4

RLA 13

1 A monogamous couple, who are married and live together. It is likely they will have children or intend to.

2 *For:* society shouldn't judge the morality of a family based upon the sex of the couple, instead it should be based upon the love and security children receive within the family unit. *Against:* some evidence suggests that homosexuals are highly promiscuous.

RLA 14

1 There has been an increase in the reporting of domestic violence and secondly, possibly a decrease in access to 'social networks' to help deal with individual frustrations.

2 Easier access to professionals (counsellors and therapists). Programmes which work on improving communication between couples.

RLA 15

1 It would be difficult to assess where 'smacking' has become 'hitting' or 'beating'.

2 Firstly, it would be difficult to enforce, and secondly, it could be seen as direct interference by the government into how parents 'bring up' their children.

RLA 16

1 You must summarize using your own words.

2 Firstly, they perhaps feel that their victim may not find them attractive, and secondly, it may give them a sense of 'power' over their victim.

RLA 17

1 You must summarize using your own words.

2 It could suggest that rape is a 'natural' male behaviour. This would imply that perpetrators couldn't help their behaviour.

RLA 18

1 Counselling, sex therapy and education and training.

2 It provides couples and individuals with understanding and practical help. It allows people a safe environment to discuss their relationship concerns in a non-threatening and non-judgemental way.

RLA 19

1 They could provide a 'secure base' during periods of difficulty. They could provide a 'focal point' to come and discuss relationship problems. They can make people feel as though they belong to something, and that they are valued and needed.

2 Firstly, many older neighbourhoods have been 'cleared' to make way for modern estates. These tend to neglect building 'focal points' where the community can meet. Secondly, people are far more mobile today, meaning they often live far away from family and friends.

RLA 20

1 You feel less inhibited in saying what you really feel. You don't have to leave the comfort of your own home. You can leave (log off) whenever you wish.

2 You will need to identify four 'chat rooms' on the Internet, and highlight who they are aimed at, and the topics people talk about while online.

RLA 21

1 Participant observation.

2 It provides a focal point of conversation. It suggests that you are a caring individual (i.e. you care enough to look after an animal). It allows you to meet other dog owners on a regular basis (remember the importance of familiarity in attraction).

R Selected references

Chapter 1

Ainsworth, MDS, Blehar, MC, Waters, E and Wall, S (1978). *Patterns of attachment: a psychological study of the strange situation*. Hillsdale, NJ: Earlbaum.

Buss, DM (1999). *Evolutionary psychology – the new science of the mind*. Boston, MA: Alyn and Bacon.

Goodwin, R (1999). *Personal relationships across cultures*. London: Routledge.

Harlow, HF and Zimmerman, RR (1959). 'Affectional responses in the infant monkey.' *Science*, 130, pp. 421–32.

Heider, F (1958). *The psychology of interpersonal relations*. New York: Wiley.

Heider, F (1994). 'Social perception and phenomenal causality.' *Psychology review*, 51, pp. 358–74.

Heiman, JR (1975). 'The physiology of erotica: women's sexual arousal.' *Psychology Today*, 8 (11), pp. 90–94.

Homans, CG (1974). *Social behaviour: its elementary forms*. 2nd edn. New York: Harcourt Brace Jovanovich.

Likert, R (1932). 'A technique for the measurement of attitudes.' *Archives of psychology*, 22, p. 140.

Maslow, A. (1954). *Motivation and personality*. New York: Harper and Row.

Moir, A and Jessel, D (1989). *Brain sex – the real difference between men and women*. London: Mandarin.

Newcombe, TM (1971). 'Dyadic balance as a source of clues about interpersonal attraction.' In Murstein, BI (ed.), *Theories of attraction and love*. New York: Springer.

Rubin, Z (1973). *Liking and loving*. New York: Holt Rinehart and Winston.

Singh, D (1993). 'Adaptive significance of waist-to-hip ratio and female attractiveness.' *Journal of personality and social psychology*, 65, pp. 293–307.

Tajfel, H and Turner, J (1979). 'An integrative theory of intergroup conflict.' In Austin, GW and Worchel, S (eds). *The social psychology of intergroup relations*. Monterey, CA: Brooks Cole.

Chapter 2

Byrne, D (1971). *The attraction paradigm*. New York: Academic Press.

Duck, S (1992). *Human Relationships*. London: Sage.

Dunbar, R (1995). 'Are you lonesome tonight?' *New scientist*, 11 February, pp. 26–31.

Fallon, AE and Rozin, P (1985). 'Sex differences in perceptions of desirable body shapes.' *Journal of abnormal psychology*, 94, pp. 102–5.

Fisher, HE (1992). *Anatomy of Love*. New York: WW Norton.

Kenrick, DT and Keefe, RC (1992). 'Age preferences in mates reflect sex difference in reproductive strategies.' *Behaviour and brain sciences*, 15, 75–133.

Kenrick, DT, Groth, GE, Trost, MR and Sadalla, EK (1993). 'Integrating evolutionary and social exchange perspectives on relationships. Effects of gender, self appraisal and involvement level on mate selection.' *Journal of personality and social psychology*, 64, pp. 951–69.

McKinstry, B and Wang, J (1991). 'Putting on the style. What patients think of the way their doctor dresses.' *British journal of general practice*, 41, pp. 275–8.

Miller, CT, Rothblum, ED, Barbour, L, Brand, PA and Felicio, D (1990). 'Social interactions of obese and nonobese women.' *Journal of personality*, 58, pp. 365–80.

Murstein, BI (1972). 'Physical attractiveness and marital choice.' *Journal of personality and social psychology*, 22 (1), pp. 8–12.

Rosenthal, R and Jacobson, L (1968). *Pygmalion in the classroom*. New York: Holt, Rhinehart and Winston.

Ross, LD (1977). 'Problems in the interpretation of "self-serving" asymmetries in causal attribution: comments on Stephan *et al.*' Paper. *Sociometry*, 40, pp. 112–14.

Thornhill, R and Moeller, AP (1997). 'Developmental stability, disease and medicine.' *Biological review*, 72, pp. 497–548.

Van Sommers, P (1988). *Jealousy – what is it and who feels it?* Harmondsworth: Penguin.

Walster, E, Aronson, E, Abrahams, D and Rottman, L (1966). 'Importance of physical attractiveness in dating behaviour.' *Journal of personality and social psychology*, 4, pp. 508–16.

Winch, RF (1958). *Mate selections: a study of complementary needs*. New York: Harper.

Zajonc, RB (1968). 'Attitudinal effects on mere

exposure.' *Journal of personality and social psychology*, monograph supplement, 9, part 2, pp. 1–27.

Chapter 3

Diamond, M (1992) *Sexwatching*. BCA edn.

Hamer, D and Copeland, P (1999). *Living with our genes*. London: Pan.

Hendrick, C and Hendrick, SS (1986). 'A theory and method of love.' *Journal of personality and social psychology*, 50, pp. 392–402.

Jourard, SM (1966). 'An exploratory study of body accessibility.' *British journal of social and clinical psychology*, 5, pp. 221–31.

Kiecolt-Glaser, JK and Glaser, R (1986). 'Psychological influences on immunity.' *Psychosomatics*, 27, pp. 621–4.

Kinsey, AC, Pomeroy, WB, Martin, CE and Gebhard, PH (1953). *Sexual behaviour in the human female*. Philadelphia: Saunders.

Rycroft, C (1985). *Psychoanalysis and beyond*. London: Hogarth Press.

Sternberg, RJ (1986). 'A triangular theory of love.' *Psychological review*, 93, pp. 119–35.

Zillman, D (1984). *Connections between sex and aggression*. Hillsdale, NJ: Earlbaum.

Chapter 4

Berkowitz, L (1966). 'On not being able to aggress.' *British journal of clinical and social psychology*, 5, pp. 130–39.

Goldberg, D, Benjamin, S and Creed, F (1994). *Psychiatry in medical practice*. London: Routledge.

Holmes, TH and Rahe, RH (1967). 'The social readjustment rating scale.' *Journal of psychosomatic research*, 11, pp. 213–18.

Lerner, M J (1980). *The belief in a just world: a fundamental delusion*. New York: Plenum.

Maccoby, EE and Jacklin, CW (1974). *The psychology of sex differences*. Stanford, CA: Stanford University Press.

Martin, P (1997). *The sickening mind – brain, behaviour, immunity and disease*. London: HarperCollins.

Mead, M (1935). *Sex and temperament in three primitive societies*. New York: Dell.

Sarrel, P and Masters, W (1982). 'Sexual molestation of men by women.' *Archives of sexual behaviour*, 11, pp. 117–32.

Satir, V (1967). 'Conjoint family therapy'. *Science and behaviour*. Palo Alto.

① Index

A

Abstinence 65–6
Adoption 76–8
Adultery 49–50
Affiliation 2–3
AIDS 72–3
Animism 2
Attachment 4, 14–17, 48
Attraction 10, 23, 24, 26, 27, 28, 32, 35, 36, 37, 38, 40, 41, 45

B

Babytalk 15
Beauty 28–34
Bereavement 87–8
Bisexuality 66
Bonding 17

C

Child abuse 81, 82
Cohabitation 74–5
Communes 75
Complementarity 37
Co-operation 9
Couples therapy 88–9
Cuteness 16

D

Date rape 83–4
Disability 87
Divorce 47–9
Domestic violence 78–81
Dress code 39–40

E

Ethics in research 7–8
Excitation transfer 58–9

F

Face shape 16
Fallibility 38, 45
Familiarity 37, 45
Family stress 85–6
Family therapy 89–90
Fundamental attribution error 26–7

G

Gay couple 61, 76–8
Gay gene 69
Glasses 40

H

Height 30–1, 41
Hermits 65, 75–6
Heterosexuality 66
Hierarchy of Needs 3–4
HIV 34, 72
Homosexuality 66–71
Hormones 11–13, 69–70
House clearance 91
Hsitrib tribe 32–3, 51
Hunting 9–10

I

Illness 87
Immune system 11, 19, 63
Incest 81
Infanticide 13, 82
Infidelity 20
Internet 91, 92–3, 94
Intimacy 3, 4, 36, 52, 53, 54, 55, 56, 65
Isolated religious groups 75–6

J

Jealousy 49–51

K

Kibbutz 75
Kissing 55–6

L

Lesbianism 66, 67–8, 70–1
Likert scale 5
Loneliness 90–1
Love 3, 4, 5, 15, 56–7, 59–60

M

Marriage 44–5, 60–5
Matching hypothesis 35–6
Mating 18, 20, 33
Monogamy 64

N

Names 23, 40
Nature–nurture debate (homosexuality) 71
Needs 2–3, 24
Non-verbal communication (NVC) 6, 38–9

O

Observations 6
Oneida commune 75
Oxytocin 13

P

Paternity uncertainty 18–19
Personal 'ads' 41–2
Pets 15, 94–5
Pheromones 10–11, 56
Polyandry 64
Polygamy 64–5
Polygyny 64
Premature babies 17–18
Proxemics 52–3
Punishment 22–3

R

Rape 82–5
Reciprocity 23–4
Reinforcement 22, 23, 24
Relate 88
Relationships:
    balance theory 20–2
    biological theories of 8
    breakdown of 45, 46–7
    communal 4–5
    economic theories 24
    equity theory 25, 37, 46
    evolutionary theories of 8–9
    exchange 4, 24–5
    learning theory 22, 80

    maintaining 42–4
    multiple 4
    primary 1, 4
    relationship therapy 88
    secondary 1, 4
Research methods 5
Rohypnol 84
Romantic love 15
Routine 43

S

Secure base 14–15
Self disclosure 40–1
Self-esteem 3, 5, 23, 34–5, 38, 47
Self-fulfilling prophecy 27
Semantic differential 5–6
Sexual disorders 12
Similarity 36, 44, 45
Smacking children 81
Social identification 2
Social support 51
Sociometry 7
Surrogate fathers 77
Survey 6–7

T

Thinness 32
Touch 17–18, 52–4
Triangular theory of love 59–60

V

Virtual neighbourhood 93

W

Walking style 40

Z

Zulu marriage 64